VACCINES

Medical Marvels

VACCINES
by Carol Hand

Content Consultant

Jonah B. Sacha, PhD
Vaccine & Gene Therapy Institute
Oregon Health & Science University

✚ Credits

Published by ABDO Publishing Company, PO Box 398166, Minneapolis, MN 55439. Copyright © 2014 by Abdo Consulting Group, Inc. International copyrights reserved in all countries. No part of this book may be reproduced in any form without written permission from the publisher. The Essential Library™ is a trademark and logo of ABDO Publishing Company.

Printed in the United States of America,
North Mankato, Minnesota
062013
092013

 THIS BOOK CONTAINS AT LEAST 10% RECYCLED MATERIALS.

Editor: Arnold Ringstad
Series Designer: Craig Hinton

Photo credits: Alexander Raths/Shutterstock Images, cover; Andrey Burmakin/Shutterstock Images, cover; Sebastian Kaulitzki/Shutterstock Images, cover; Shutterstock Images, cover; Bettmann/Corbis/AP Images, 7; Matty Zimmerman/AP Images, 9; AP Images, 11, 24, 67, 78; Henry Griffin/AP Images, 15; Jean-Marc Bouju/AP Images, 19; Science Photo Library/Custom Medical Stock Photo, 20; Monkey Business Images/Shutterstock Images, 26; J. Scott Appelwhite/AP Images, 29; iStockphoto/Thinkstock, 31; North Wind Picture Archives, 33, 35; Joe Raedle/Getty Images, 39; Ross D. Franklin/AP Images, 41; Imagechina/AP Images, 44; CDC, 47, 53, 56; Altaf Qadri/AP Images, 51; Seth Wenig/AP Images, 59; Michael Rosenfeld/picture-alliance/dpa/AP Images, 63; James Gathany/CDC, 64; David Massey/Daytona Beach News-Journal/AP Images, 70; David Cheskin/Press Association/AP Images, 75; Reed Saxon/AP Images, 81; Jose Luis Magana/AP Images, 84; Peter Endig/picture-alliance/dpa/AP Images, 87; Jacquelyn Marin/AP Images, 89; Bill Grimshaw/AP Images, 91; Pete Souza, 93; Charles Dharapak/AP Images, 95; Kenneth Lambert/AP Images, 96

Library of Congress Control Number: 2013932977
Cataloging-in-Publication Data

Hand, Carol.
 Vaccines / Carol Hand.
  p. cm. -- (Medical marvels)
 Includes bibliographical references and index.
 ISBN 978-1-61783-905-4
 1. Vaccination--Juvenile literature. 2. Vaccines--Juvenile literature. 3. Communicable diseases--Prevention--History--Juvenile literature. I. Title.
 614.4/7--dc23

                              2013932977

Contents

Polio: Scourge of Summer

It was 1916. Heat rose from the pavements of New York City as kids looked forward to a lazy summer of playing ball, swimming, and hanging out with friends. Parents went about their daily routines. Then people, mostly children, began to come down with a mysterious illness. Most cases mimicked colds or flu, causing sore throats, headaches, and chills, but no lasting damage. Sometimes people had a stiff neck or sensitivity to light, which also disappeared after a short time. But in a few cases, people lost the use of legs, arms, and even the muscles used for breathing and swallowing. One day a child might be picnicking and splashing in the surf with her family. By the next day she would be completely paralyzed. Polio had arrived.

During the 1916 epidemic, polio killed approximately one-quarter of the people it struck.

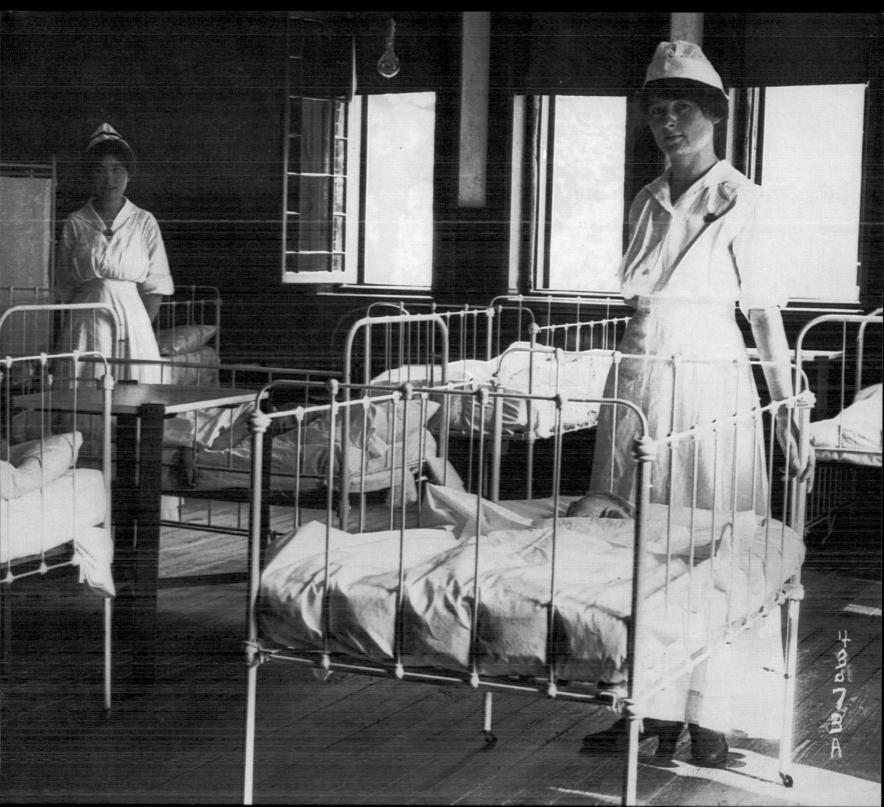

> "The fear of polio was a fear of something you had no defense against, something that hit without logic or reason. Yesterday, it was the man down the block. Today it could be you or your children."[2]
>
> —Larry Alexander, polio victim, 1954

In one frightening summer, approximately 27,000 people in the United States contracted polio. Approximately 6,000 died. More than 9,000 cases and 2,343 deaths were reported in New York City alone.[1] Many sufferers were left paralyzed, with twisted, crippled limbs.

The Spread of Polio

Polio has been around since prehistory, but medical science first described it in 1789. The disease appeared in the United States in 1894. In 1908, Dr. Karl Landsteiner and Dr. Erwin Popper identified its cause: poliovirus. Ironically, improved sanitation may have led to the rise of polio as a serious disease. When sanitation was poor, infants were exposed to small amounts of the virus in polluted drinking water. The infants produced antibodies to defend against the virus. Combined with immunity gained from their mothers' milk, this protected them. But with cleaner living conditions, babies were no longer exposed to the virus. When they first encountered it as older children, they had no defenses. They were often stricken with severe, paralytic polio.

Between 1916 and 1955, summer was a season of fear in the United States. The number of polio cases varied from year to year, but the disease remained a constant threat. Because it was contagious, people limited contact with others. Children were kept at home. People avoided swimming pools, beaches, playgrounds, and public water fountains. Public health officials attempted to use methods useful against other contagious diseases such as typhoid and tuberculosis. They quarantined the houses

+ Forms of Polio

Asymptomatic polio: shows no symptoms; includes approximately 95 percent of cases [3]

Abortive polio: shows symptoms of a mild respiratory infection (fever, sore throat, and diarrhea); patients usually recover completely

Nonparalytic polio: occurs in 1 to 5 percent of cases; symptoms include fever, stiff neck, light sensitivity, and mild temporary paralysis; most patients recover completely [4]

Paralytic polio: occurs in 0.1 to 2 percent of cases; the virus attacks nerves affecting muscle movement (arm and leg muscles); when it affects breathing muscles, patients may die [5]

of people with polio. They put up warning posters and flushed streets with water. But polio did not go away.

Facing the Fear

Polio was not the greatest killer of the time. Diseases such as tuberculosis, pneumonia, and influenza killed many more people. But no one was sure exactly how polio spread, how to prevent it, or how to treat it. It seemed to strike at random. Fear of polio was worsened by the way polio sufferers were treated. Families were split apart as affected children were taken to hospitals and placed in polio wards. News articles showed families outside hospital wards communicating with their children by tapping on windows. Paralyzed children required constant nursing care. Those whose breathing muscles were affected were placed in iron lungs. An iron lung is an airtight metal cylinder that encloses the whole body except for the head. Inside, changes in air pressure

Living inside an iron lung could be a traumatizing experience for young children.

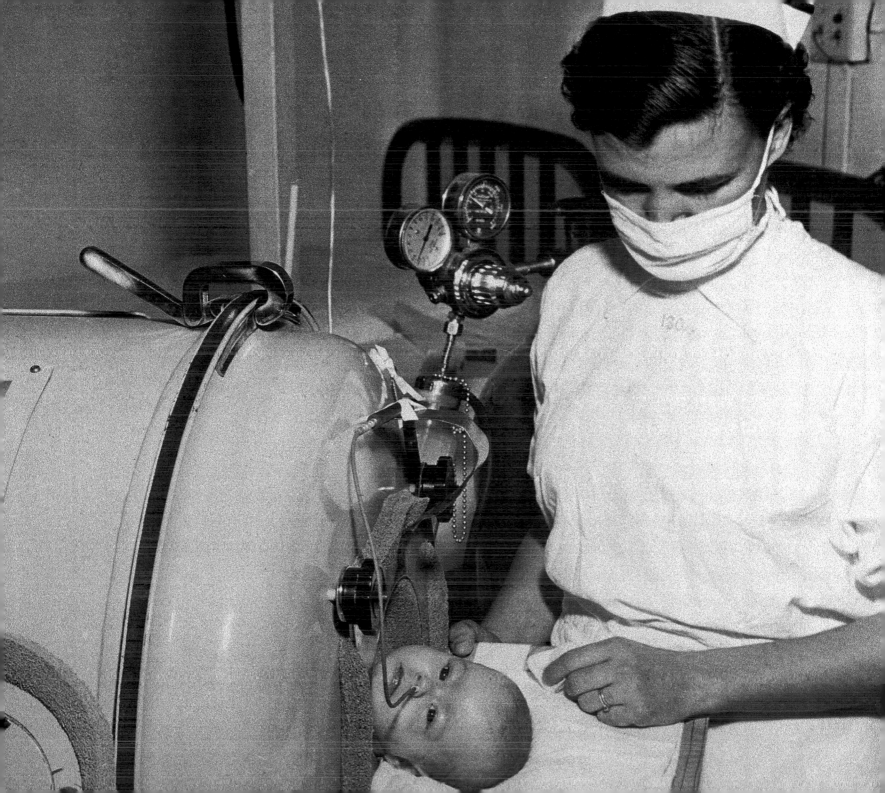

force the patient's nonfunctional lungs to breathe in and out, but the patient could not move. Even worse, the disease caused constant pain. But pain medications were not allowed because they interfered with breathing.

Polio seemed to affect mostly children, so at first it was called infantile paralysis. However, it also affected teens and adults. Its scientific name is poliomyelitis. *Polio-* comes from the Greek word for "gray". The ending *-myelitis* refers to an inflammation of the gray matter of the spinal cord. The name was shortened to "polio." The disease swept through towns and cities during summer and receded during winter. Cases increased in the late 1940s and early 1950s. The disease peaked in 1952 when 57,879 people were affected and 21,269 were paralyzed.[6]

Polio survivors were often targets of discrimination and had difficulties in everyday life. Some campaigned for disability rights to help reverse these problems.

Franklin Delano Roosevelt, president of the United States from 1932 until his death in 1945, became a role model of courage in the fight against polio. Roosevelt was stricken at age 39 by the symptoms of polio. He lost the use of his legs but refused to let his disability stop him from living a full, rich life. He formed a foundation, the March of Dimes, to raise money for polio treatment and development of a vaccine. A 2003 study concluded Roosevelt probably suffered from a different rare disorder rather than polio. But at the time, he was thought to have polio. His leadership in the fight against the disease was crucial.

Finding a Vaccine

Polio is incurable, so scientists instead tried to prevent people from getting it in the first place. This required a vaccine, a substance made with all or part of a disease-causing organism. Vaccines help people's immune systems learn how to fight a disease. Polio vaccine research proceeded on two fronts. One group, led by Dr. Jonas Salk, worked on a vaccine using an inactivated poliovirus. Another group, led by Dr. Albert Sabin, worked with a weakened virus.

Salk's killed-virus vaccine was considered very safe because it could not give people polio. But some people

+ Roosevelt Fights Polio

Roosevelt used a wheelchair in private but refused to let his disability be photographed. During his presidency, he gave speeches standing up by locking his leg braces and supporting himself against a lectern or another person. In 1938, he formed the National Foundation for Infantile Paralysis. Entertainer Eddie Cantor publicized the foundation by encouraging citizens to start a "March of Dimes." This was a pun on the name of a popular series of news films called "The March of Time." In the year it was founded, people sent more than 2.6 million dimes to the White House to help fund a polio cure.[7]

The Cutter Incident

Two weeks after the Salk polio vaccinations began, cases of polio began to appear in children who had received Salk's vaccine. Somehow the virus in the vaccine was still alive. The bad vaccine was traced to Cutter Laboratories in California. Salk had provided detailed instructions for preparing the vaccine, but Cutter Laboratories did not follow them precisely. The lab's production facility was crude and unsanitary. At least 220,000 people received the tainted vaccine. Seventy thousand became ill, 164 suffered severe paralysis, and ten died.[10] The Cutter Incident was a major setback in the fight against polio and hurt Salk's reputation, even though he was not at fault. But it also led to major reforms in vaccine safety regulation.

feared it would provide only a short-lived immunity. Others feared it would always contain a small amount of live virus. But Salk made his vaccine very carefully. He was so confident in its safety he injected 161 people, including schoolchildren and his own family, in 1952 and 1953.[8] These successful tests were followed by a large-scale trial in 1954. Parents signed up 1.8 million children to be "polio pioneers."[9] The trial showed Salk's vaccine to be effective, and it was licensed for use on April 12, 1955. Salk became a national hero.

Still, Albert Sabin was convinced his live, weakened virus was necessary to give permanent immunity. After patients are vaccinated with his oral vaccine, the weakened virus is released in their feces and enters the water supply. This boosts immunity of others, even those who have not been vaccinated. However, because the vaccine contains live virus, there is always some risk of people contracting the disease from the vaccine. After Salk's

Jonas Salk, *left*, and Albert Sabin, *right*, worked tirelessly to develop a polio vaccine in the 1950s.

Polio Before and After Vaccines

Year	Number of Polio Cases
1951	28,386
1952	57, 879
1953	35,592
1954	38,476
1955*	28,985
1956	15,140
1957	5,485
1958	5,787
1959	8,425
1960	3,190
1961**	1,312
1962	940
1963	449
1964	112
1965	72
1966	113
1967	41[13]

*Salk's vaccine was introduced on April 12.

**Sabin's vaccine was introduced on August 17.

vaccine was approved, Sabin continued to work on his vaccine.

Sabin's vaccine was licensed in 1961. By then, Salk's vaccine had already reduced polio cases by 97 percent from 1952 levels.[11] Between 1963 and 1999, Sabin's oral polio vaccine (OPV) replaced Salk's injected polio vaccine (IPV) around the world. But the live Sabin vaccine occasionally becomes strong enough to cause polio. Beginning in 1999, Salk's killed vaccine was again used in the United States. Together, the two vaccines have wiped out polio in the United States. Since 1966, there have been fewer than ten paralytic cases per year.[12] The last known naturally occurring case was recorded in 1998.

The Age of Vaccines

The polio vaccine was not the first vaccine invented. Vaccines against smallpox had been used for more than a century before polio epidemics began. Vaccination of children against infectious diseases, including polio, improved life expectancy throughout the 1900s. Today, vaccines are recommended for 17 diseases.[14]

Vaccination is particularly important because new strains of diseases continue to emerge. Rapidly responding to new diseases with new vaccines can prevent illnesses and even save lives. Additionally, since people are increasingly mobile, diseases can travel farther and faster than ever before. New vaccination technologies will be a vital part of public health outreach throughout the world in the coming years. And new generations must continue to be vaccinated against diseases such as polio to prevent these diseases from reemerging.

Introducing Vaccines

Throughout history, one of the greatest threats to human health has been infectious disease. In 1900, the three leading causes of death in the United States included two infectious diseases, pneumonia and tuberculosis, as well as diarrhea caused by infection.[1] By 1997, three of the leading causes were heart disease, cancer, and stroke, none of which is infectious.[2] During the twentieth century, infectious diseases in the developed world were tamed in large part thanks to one medical breakthrough: vaccines.

The Human Immune System

The human immune system is a complex disease-fighting system spread throughout the body. It consists of special organs, cells, and molecules that work together to protect the body. They are

One of the symptoms of the deadly infectious disease tuberculosis is dramatic weight loss.

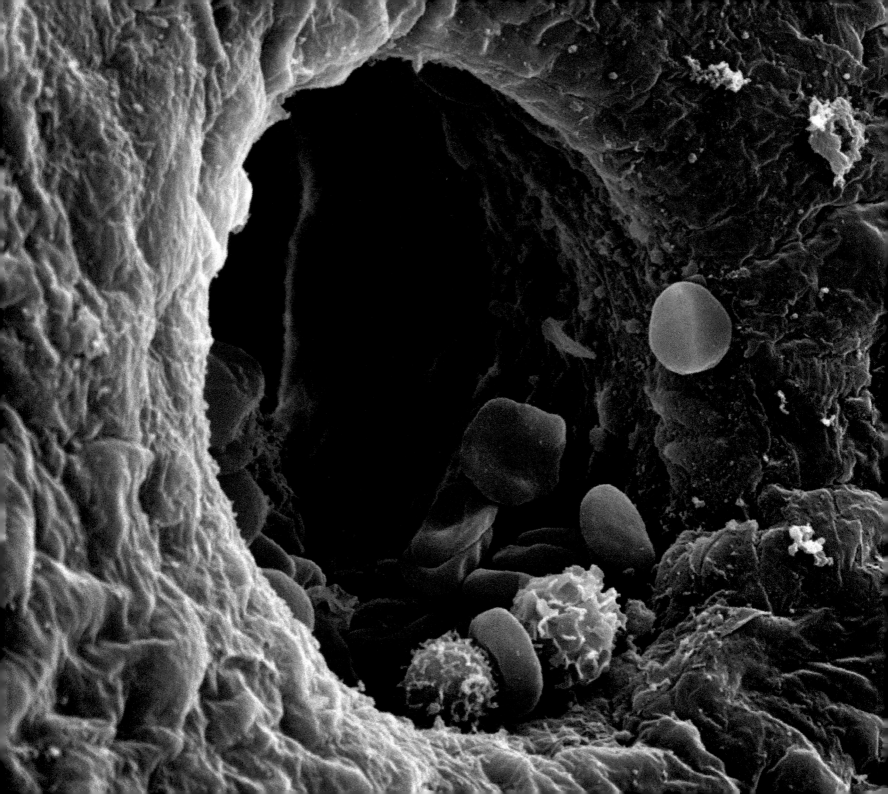

programmed to attack and destroy foreign organisms or substances, such as bacteria, viruses, or toxins. Toxins include the venom from snakes, bees, and other animals. These foreign substances are called antigens. The skin—the largest organ in the human body—forms a barrier that stops most antigens. Those that do enter the body encounter a group of disease-fighting cells and molecules.

Leukocytes, commonly known as white blood cells, are the body's immune cells. They travel through the blood and lymph fluids and collect in lymph nodes throughout the body. These lymph nodes help form the lymphatic system, which helps circulate and recycle blood through the body. Different types of leukocytes have different functions. Macrophages are nonspecific—they attack anything foreign. This means they can react to antigens very rapidly. Along with the skin, these leukocytes provide natural immunity—the kind of immunity a person is born with. B lymphocytes and T lymphocytes, known as B cells and T cells, are leukocytes that react more slowly. They provide long-term acquired immunity, called immune memory—the kind of immunity obtained after birth by exposure to antigens.

The Immune Response and Vaccines

Acquired immunity develops when the body is exposed to a disease-causing organism, called a pathogen. When a body encounters disease in nature, the body may be exposed to large quantities of the disease organism. During the first encounter, the immune system may be overwhelmed, making the person ill. The immune system mobilizes to destroy invading pathogens. Some B and T cells form

Leukocytes, or white blood cells, travel through blood vessels alongside red blood cells, which distribute oxygen throughout the body.

+ Active versus Passive Immunity

In active immunity, exposure to a disease activates the body's immune system, which then makes its own antibodies. In passive immunity, the person receives someone else's antibodies. These loaned antibodies prevent the disease, but immunity lasts only a few weeks or months and memory cells are not formed. Immunity passed to a baby in its mother's breast milk provides natural passive immunity. Artificial passive immunity is induced by injection of purified antibodies from immune people or animals. It may be used after exposure to prevent certain diseases, such as rabies. It is quick acting and beneficial to people with weakened immune systems.

memory cells in reaction to the disease. Memory cells enable the immune system to remember that particular disease-causing organism. The next time the organism is encountered, the immune system is able to mobilize quickly. The memory B cells will produce high quantities of antibodies targeted against the organism. Antibodies attach to matching antigens on disease organisms and help destroy them. Each type of antibody binds only to its specific antigen. This process destroys organisms and antigens floating free in the blood and lymph fluid. T cells also bind to antigens, but unlike B cells they destroy disease-causing organisms that hide inside cells.

Vaccines assist the immune system by providing an artificial form of acquired immunity. A vaccine contains all or part of the disease-causing organism. Giving a vaccine before the disease is encountered in nature deliberately exposes the body to small amounts of the antigen. The organism has been killed or weakened, so it does not actually cause the disease. But, just as in natural exposure, the antigen's presence stimulates the immune system. It produces antibodies to fight the disease and memory cells to remember it. In every future encounter with the disease, a vaccinated person will be able to quickly produce large quantities of antibodies against it. These antibodies will prevent him or her from becoming ill.

The Language of Vaccines

Immunization is the process of building up immunity to a disease by taking a vaccine. The words *immunization* and *immunize* relate to the immune system, the body's system responsible for keeping us healthy.

Smallpox, also known by its Latin name *variola*, was the first disease people seriously tried to prevent. Before a vaccine was developed, smallpox killed up to 30 percent of those it infected.[3] The symptoms included severe fever and pain, as well as marks on the skin called pox or pustules. An early attempt at prevention was through variolation, likely first practiced in India or China more than 1,000 years ago. In this process, a knife was used to scratch fresh material from smallpox pustules into a person's skin. This caused a local infection that gave the person immunity. The terms *vaccine* and *vaccination* were coined in 1800 to describe the process British scientist Edward Jenner used to induce smallpox immunity. These terms are based on the Latin word *vacca*, or "cow," because Jenner discovered that variolation using the milder cowpox virus also induced smallpox immunity. Variolation

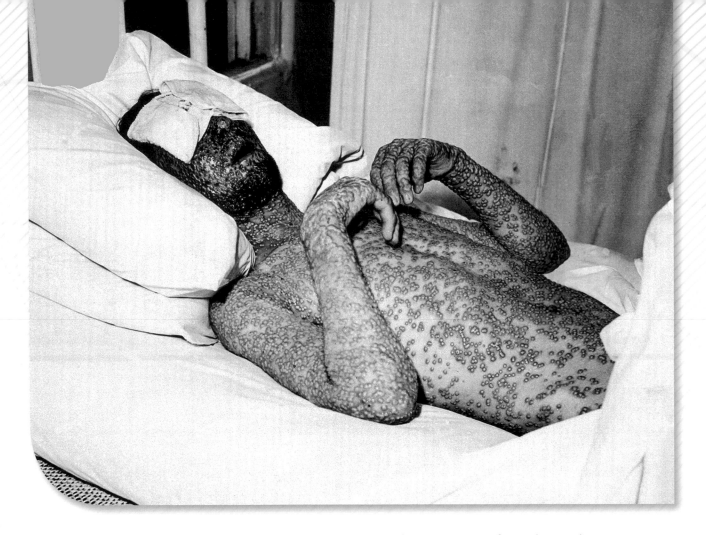

and vaccination are both forms of inoculation, the general term for the process of introducing disease material into a healthy person to create immunity.

Smallpox had been infecting and killing people for thousands of years before medical technology advanced far enough to prevent it.

Today, the terms *immunization*, *inoculation*, and *vaccination* are often used interchangeably. However, vaccines are no longer crude concoctions. Doses are purified and precisely measured. Many vaccines now contain only the exact antigens needed to stimulate the production of antibodies. Most vaccinations today are done by injection, although some are given orally or as a nasal spray.

Reasons to Immunize

Immunization protects the life and health of individuals. In the past, parents lived in constant fear of infectious diseases taking their children. Once, the only way to become immune was to have the disease and survive it. Today, childhood immunizations prevent individuals from contracting diseases throughout life. This decreases their risk of complications and death.

Not all vaccinations are given in childhood. Immunization also protects against transmission of diseases during travel. Yellow fever, which causes severe and fatal bleeding from the mouth, eyes, and organs, is still prevalent in parts of Africa and South America. People visiting these areas are vaccinated before they leave to prevent contracting and spreading this disease.

Immunization also protects society. Without immunization, the likelihood is very high infected people will transmit a disease to others, causing an epidemic. When most members of a community are immunized, disease transmission is much less likely. Even if a few people get the disease, the disease's

spread will halt when it reaches an immunized person. This protection of entire communities by vaccinating large percentages of the community is called herd immunity.

Finally, immunization protects the health of future generations. Some people assume once levels of a disease decline in a population, immunization is no longer necessary. But the process must be maintained to keep the disease at low levels. Unless the disease is completely extinct in nature, decreased vaccination rates are likely to result in outbreaks. So far, only one human disease, smallpox, is thought to be fully eradicated in nature. Diseases that have nearly vanished in the United States today, such as polio and diphtheria, still exist elsewhere. Vaccination campaigns must continue if these diseases, too, are to be eradicated.

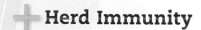

Herd Immunity

Herd immunity protects even unvaccinated members of a community. If most people are vaccinated, unvaccinated people are less likely to be exposed to the disease and an outbreak is less likely. But if vaccination rates drop below a certain percentage, herd immunity is lost and outbreaks can occur. In England in the late 1990s, MMR (measles, mumps, rubella) vaccination rates dropped from more than 90 percent to less than 80 percent. This is below the threshold for protection against measles. In 1998, only 56 cases of measles occurred in England and Wales, but in 2008, there were 1,348 cases.[4]

Most vaccines are given during childhood, giving patients lifelong protection against many diseases.

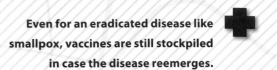

Even for an eradicated disease like smallpox, vaccines are still stockpiled in case the disease reemerges.

What Would Happen if Vaccination Stopped?

A worldwide total of 100 million children per year are vaccinated against common diseases such as measles and polio. But 25 million children do not receive the necessary vaccinations. Every year, approximately 2.4 million children die from diseases that could have been prevented by a vaccine. The toll accounts for 14 percent of deaths in children under age five worldwide.[5]

Measles in the United States has decreased by 99 percent since vaccination began. But it would rapidly increase again if vaccination ended. The disease is highly infectious. More than 90 percent of people who are not immunized get the disease if exposed. It is often brought into the United States by international travelers, and it spreads rapidly in developing countries. In 1999, according to the World Health Organization (WHO), nearly 900,000 people in developing countries died of measles. Worldwide, approximately 2.7 million measles deaths per year would occur without vaccinations.[6]

Since the WHO agreed in 1988 to attempt to eradicate polio around the world, cases have dropped dramatically. In that year, 350,000 cases were reported; by 2012, the number was only 187.[7] But polio is still a danger. Until recently, polio outbreaks were thought to be limited to three nations: Afghanistan, Pakistan, and Nigeria. However, in November 2010, an outbreak was confirmed in three more African countries. It attacked mostly young adults who had not been fully immunized. The outbreak led to a campaign to vaccinate 3 million at-risk people.[8]

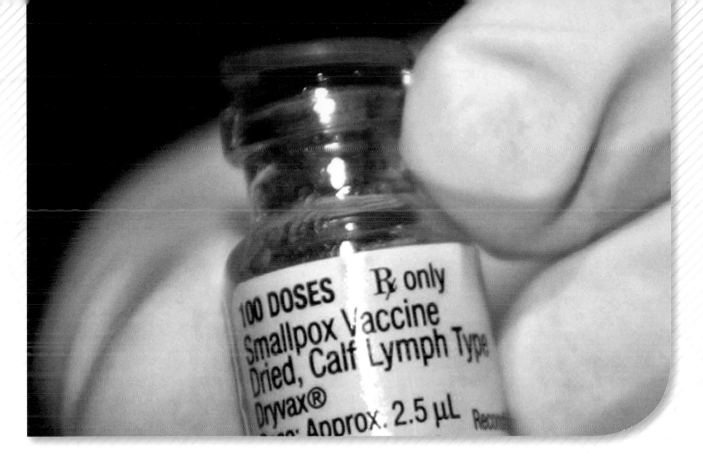

Many other diseases in the United States have been drastically reduced by vaccination. These include chicken pox, diphtheria, *Haemophilus influenzae* type B (Hib), hepatitis B, meningitis, pertussis, pneumococcal disease, rubella, and tetanus. For example, in 1921, there were 206,000 cases of diphtheria and 15,520 deaths. A vaccine was introduced in 1923, and in 2001, only two cases were reported.[9] However, these diseases continue to exist in the United States and other countries. Vaccines will continue to be essential to a healthy human future.

The Search for Vaccines

In 1900, few people lived past age 50. By 2011, life spans rose dramatically worldwide. Life spans in East Asia increased from less than 45 years in 1950 to more than 74 years in 2011.[1] Previously, most people died from infectious and parasitic diseases, which affect all age groups. Today, noninfectious diseases and chronic conditions such as heart disease and cancer kill most people. These primarily affect older age groups. Most children and young adults now survive into adulthood.

In the 1900s, sanitation improvements such as clean drinking water slowed infections and decreased death rates. Public health campaigns were also launched to vaccinate people against diseases including smallpox, polio, and measles. But before that, diseases swept through

Vaccines have been a major factor in the massive increase in life expectancy in the 1900s. More and more people are healthy into their 70s and 80s.

populations, killing rich and poor, powerful and powerless alike. They affected the outcomes of wars and changed societies and economies.

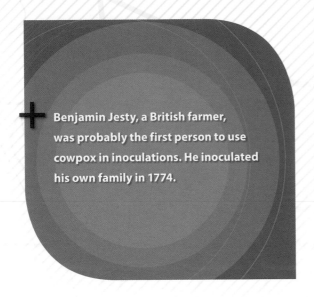

Benjamin Jesty, a British farmer, was probably the first person to use cowpox in inoculations. He inoculated his own family in 1774.

The Fight Against Smallpox

Smallpox had a major impact on populations. It spread rapidly, often through travel. Throughout the 1600s, European settlers infected Native American populations in Canada and New England. Many settlers died, but the disease was particularly deadly to Native Americans, who had never encountered it.

Outbreaks of smallpox and other diseases took their toll on colonial America during the 1600s and 1700s. A 1735 diphtheria epidemic killed 32 percent of children under age ten.[2]

In the 1700s, variolation began to control smallpox in Europe and North America. It had been used in Africa, India, and China long before that. Lady Mary Montagu, an English writer, brought the process from Turkey to England in 1721. Still, 2 to 3 percent of variolated people died, started another epidemic, or developed other diseases (such as tuberculosis or syphilis) transmitted by the procedure.[3]

In 1721, variolation reached North America. The first inoculations took place in Boston, Massachusetts. A study published by Cotton Mather on the effectiveness of the process helped spread its use. General George Washington ordered mandatory inoculation of all American troops during the Revolutionary War (1775–1783) in 1777.

The drive to control smallpox intensified in the nineteenth century. Edward Jenner, a British physician and naturalist, was not the first to use cowpox in inoculations. But he was the first to carry out scientific experiments proving that cowpox inoculation prevented smallpox. Jenner's procedure,

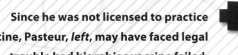

called vaccination, reached the United States in 1800. In 1813, Congress established the National Vaccine Agency to supply all US citizens with smallpox vaccine. By the 1950s, smallpox had been eradicated in much of Europe and North America. However, it was still epidemic in 63 countries.[4] In 1967, the WHO began a campaign to eradicate it. In 1980, it declared smallpox eradicated and vaccinations were discontinued. So far, smallpox is the only infectious human disease to be eradicated worldwide.

Study Begins on Other Diseases

During the 1800s, not all doctors and researchers focused on smallpox. Within a few decades, the bacteria and viruses responsible for some of the most feared diseases were identified. Work began to develop vaccines for these diseases. During this time, epidemics continued in

Jenner's Experiment

On May 14, 1796, Edward Jenner took fresh material from a cowpox pustule on a dairymaid's hand and used it to inoculate eight-year-old James Phipps. Phipps developed a mild fever and soreness in his armpits. Nine days later, he felt cold and lost his appetite, but the symptoms lasted only one day. In July, Jenner inoculated Phipps again, this time with fresh smallpox material. The boy did not develop smallpox, and Jenner concluded he had been immunized. Later, Jenner performed the same experiment on many other people. He published his results, naming his process "vaccination."

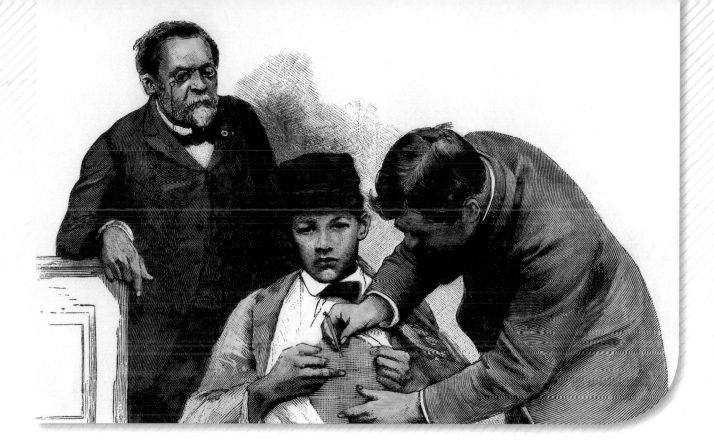

the United States and elsewhere. Cholera pandemics swept the world approximately every 20 years beginning in 1817. Two-thirds of all deaths in the American Civil War (1861–1865) were caused by infectious diseases, including measles and smallpox. In 1878, more than 13,000 people in the lower Mississippi valley died of yellow fever.[5]

Louis Pasteur was a French chemist and microbiologist. His work on infectious diseases laid the foundation for much of the modern understanding of the immune system. He developed the germ theory of disease, which states that microorganisms, or germs, cause diseases. Along with other scientists, he worked on vaccines to prevent these diseases. In 1879, he produced the first laboratory-made vaccine, which protected against chicken cholera, a disease affecting poultry. Pasteur's best-known contribution to immunology is his development of a rabies vaccine. On July 6, 1885, he successfully prevented rabies in a nine-year-old boy after the boy was bitten by a rabid dog. Pasteur's discoveries have protected millions of people from disease.

Immunization Efforts Take Off

Later in the 1800s, immunization research expanded dramatically. In 1885, Spanish physician Jaime Ferrán developed a cholera vaccine. A diphtheria antitoxin was developed in 1890 and entered production in the United States in 1895. Diphtheria cases began to decline. In 1897, German scientist Paul Ehrlich developed a standardized unit for measuring diphtheria antitoxin. Standardization made the science of vaccines more precise than ever. This was a major breakthrough in the development of vaccines.

In the early 1900s, deaths due to yellow fever and malaria slowed the construction of the Panama Canal. A massive project, the canal would connect the Atlantic and Pacific Oceans in Central America. US Army researchers proved that yellow fever was transmitted by mosquitoes and was caused by a virus. The disease was controlled using pesticide chemicals to kill mosquitoes. The last yellow fever epidemic in North America occurred in New Orleans in 1905. By then, other diseases, including polio, were beginning to increase in frequency.

By the 1920s, schoolchildren in many areas were being vaccinated against smallpox and diphtheria. Meanwhile, the search continued for other vaccines. Trials of an early polio vaccine in 1935 caused the death or paralysis of some vaccinated children. The vaccine was abandoned. Max Theiler, a Harvard University instructor, was more successful with his yellow fever vaccine. It was tested in 1936 and accepted for mass production the following year. Theiler's vaccine became the world standard for fighting the disease. And in 1939, scientists Pearl Kendrick and Grace Elderding developed a pertussis vaccine.

Vaccination campaigns and advances continued into the 1940s and 1950s. During the International Tuberculosis

Dogs Race to Save Children

In 1925, a diphtheria outbreak occurred in Nome, Alaska. On January 22, Dr. Curtis Welch sent a telegram requesting delivery of fresh antitoxin. An Anchorage hospital shipped 300,000 units of antitoxin by train to Nenana. From there, 20 teams of drivers and sled dogs battled bitterly cold temperatures for 674 miles (1,080 km) to reach Nome.[6] Many sled dogs died and some drivers suffered frostbite. The antitoxin arrived on February 2 and saved many children. Lead sled dogs Togo and Balto received national honors. Balto's statue still stands in Central Park in New York City.

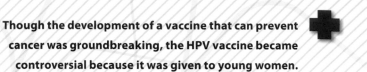

Though the development of a vaccine that can prevent cancer was groundbreaking, the HPV vaccine became controversial because it was given to young women.

Campaign, launched in 1947, millions of people across the world received a vaccine for tuberculosis. The campaign ran through 1951. By the end of the 1950s, scientists were turning the tide in the battle against polio in the United States. Salk and Sabin's successful polio vaccines were released in 1955 and 1961, respectively.

Immunization Efforts Mature

During the late 1900s, development of vaccines and immunization programs led to major declines in deaths from nine diseases: smallpox, diphtheria, tetanus, pertussis, polio, measles, mumps, rubella, and Hib. All except smallpox were on the list of vaccines recommended for children in 1990. Through 1999, 21 other vaccines were developed and licensed. Ten are recommended only in high-risk populations, while the other 11 are recommended for all US children.[7]

One of the most significant advances in vaccines came in 2006 with the introduction of the human papillomavirus (HPV) vaccine. HPV, a sexually transmitted virus, can lead to several kinds of cancers, including cervical cancer. This meant the HPV vaccine was the first vaccine to protect against the development of cancer. The vaccine crossed paths with politics shortly after it was introduced. When it became mandatory in some states, vocal politicians argued that by lowering the chance of sex leading to cervical cancer, the vaccine would make young women more likely to engage in sexual activity.

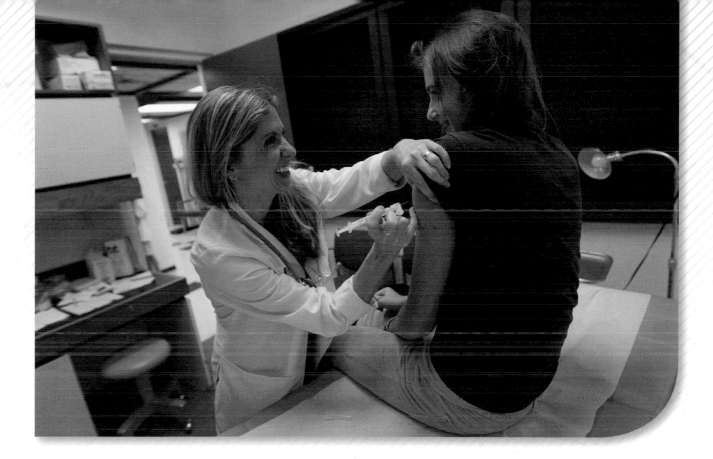

In the early 2000s, the rapid pace of vaccine development has continued. But researchers still have only a limited understanding of how vaccines work. Although side effects are rare, they limit effectiveness and help spread fear of vaccination. Outbreaks continue to occur when vaccination rates decrease or when diseases emerge or enter from outside the country. These problems, as well as the ongoing search for new vaccines, ensure that research into immunity and vaccination will remain active during the 2000s.

Types of Vaccines

On the surface, it may seem as though all vaccines are alike. A person receives an injection in childhood and receives lifelong immunity to a specific disease. But it is not that simple. Vaccine technology has expanded the types of vaccines available and made them safer and more effective. In part, this is done by carefully crafting each vaccine based on the characteristics of the pathogen.

Five Types of Vaccines

The five general categories of vaccines are as follows: vaccines with live, attenuated viruses; those with inactivated or killed viruses; toxoid vaccines; subunit vaccines; and conjugate vaccines.

One of the most commonly given live-virus vaccines is the nasal spray flu vaccine.

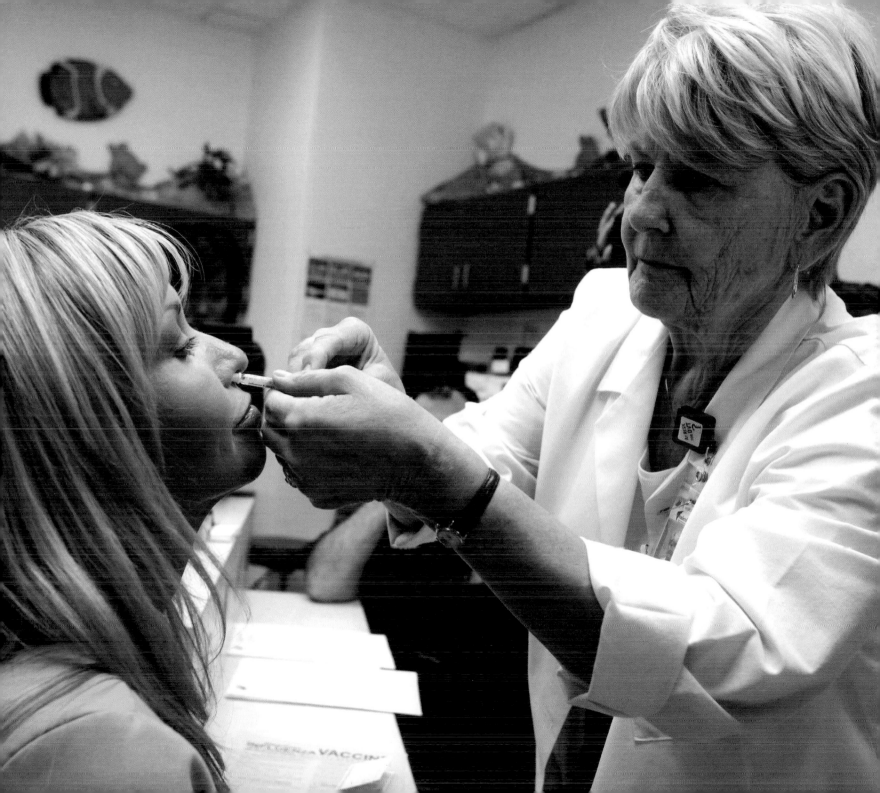

Examples of Each Vaccine Type

Vaccine Type	Vaccines on US Immunization Schedule*	Other Available Vaccines
Live, attenuated	Measles, mumps, rubella (MMR combined)	Zoster (shingles)
	Chicken pox	
	Influenza (nasal spray)	Yellow fever
	Rotavirus	
Inactivated, killed	Polio (IPV)	Rabies
	Hepatitis A	
Toxoid	Diphtheria, tetanus (part of DTaP combined)	--
Subunit or Conjugate	Hepatitis B	Human papillomavirus (HPV)
	Influenza (injection)	
	Haemophilus influenzae type b (Hib)	
	Pertussis (part of DTaP combined)	
	Pneumococcal	
	Meningococcal	

*Recommended for ages 0 to 6 years

In vaccines with live, attenuated viruses, pathogens are still alive, but are weakened. This is done by passing them through a series of cell cultures or chick embryos. With each passage, the virus becomes better able to replicate in cultures or embryos and less able to replicate in human cells. But the virus still causes an immune response and produces immunity in humans. An attenuated vaccine provides long-lasting disease protection. However, there is some danger that the virus will return to its normal virulent, or disease-causing, form. This rarely happens, but it has occurred in Sabin's OPV. For this reason, the OPV is no longer used in the United States. The process is still used for some vaccines, including the rabies vaccine.

Some vaccines are made from pathogens that have been killed or inactivated using heat or chemicals. The immune system still recognizes the pathogen, so the vaccine causes antibody production and gives the patient immunity. The term *killed* refers to living pathogens such as bacteria or fungi. *Inactivated* refers to viruses, which are not technically alive. These vaccines are safer than those made from live, attenuated viruses. Because the pathogens cannot reproduce, there is no chance they will revert to a virulent state. But the immunity these vaccines provide is short term, and booster shots may be needed. Annual flu shots contain inactivated viruses.

Sometimes a disease is caused by the toxin a bacterium produces rather than by the bacterium itself. In this case, only the toxin is needed to produce the vaccine. The toxin is inactivated with heat or a chemical, forming a toxoid. Toxoid vaccines are similar to killed or inactivated vaccines and are sometimes grouped with them. The tetanus vaccine is an example.

Subunit vaccines contain only part of the pathogen, usually a specific protein from the pathogen's outside surface. The immune system treats the protein as an antigen and makes antibodies to combat it. These vaccines can be made by removing a protein from the pathogen and injecting it alone. The

immune system then creates defenses against the protein without a doctor having to inject the entire pathogen. One example of this type of vaccine is the vaccine against hepatitis B.

In conjugate vaccines, pieces of bacteria are combined with a carrier protein to produce the vaccine. The bacterial pieces alone cannot cause illness and do not cause the immune system to

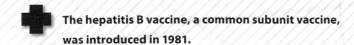
respond. But when combined with the carrier protein, they make the immune system react. Vaccines for pneumococcal bacterial infections are of this type.

Childhood and Adult Vaccines

Most vaccines are given in early childhood, from birth through age six. They are given on a schedule based on when they will be most effective. For example, the vaccine for rotavirus, the most common cause of childhood diarrhea, is given in three doses at approximately two, four, and six months of age.

Many vaccines require several doses to be most effective. This is particularly true of inactivated vaccines, such as the Hib vaccine, which protects against meningitis. Because the inactivated vaccines cause less of a response from the immune system than live vaccines, immunity to the disease eventually wears off. This is true of the DTaP vaccine for diphtheria, tetanus, and pertussis. Infants initially receive a series of four DTaP shots. A booster dose is given at four to six years and another at 11 to 12 years. Additional boosters are recommended every

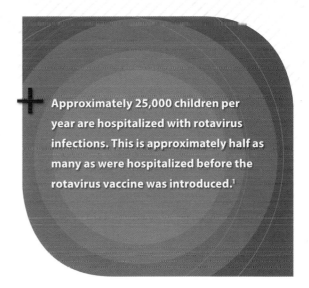

Approximately 25,000 children per year are hospitalized with rotavirus infections. This is approximately half as many as were hospitalized before the rotavirus vaccine was introduced.[1]

Childhood Vaccination Schedule

This table shows the recommended vaccination schedule for healthy children in the United States.

Vaccine	Age Given
Hepatitis B	Birth, 1–2 months, 6–18 months
Rotavirus	2 months, 4 months, 6 months
Diphtheria, tetanus, pertussis (DTaP)	2 months, 4 months, 6 months, 15–18 months, 4–6 years
Haemophilus influenzae type b (Hib)	2 months, 4 months, 6 months, 12–15 months
Pneumococcal (PCV)	2 months, 4 months, 6 months, 12–15 months
Inactivated poliovirus (IPV)	2 months, 4 months, 6–18 months, 4–6 years
Influenza	yearly after 6 months
Measles, mumps, rubella (MMR)	12–18 months, 4–6 years
Chicken pox	12–18 months, 4–6 years
Hepatitis A (dose 1)	12–23 months
Meningococcal	9 months–4–6 years[2]

ten years throughout life. A booster called Tdap may be given to teens and adults. It is used when a patient is injured in a way that might leave them vulnerable to tetanus, such as stepping on a rusty nail. Certain kinds of vaccines sometimes fail to generate enough immunity with a single dose. For these types, a second dose is required to achieve complete immunity. This is the case for the live MMR vaccine, which protects against measles, mumps, and rubella. Finally, the flu vaccine must be taken every year. Each year, scientists predict which three forms of flu will be most dangerous in the coming year. These are the types that are targeted in each year's vaccine, and they can change annually.

Some vaccines are given during the late childhood or teen years. These include vaccines for meningococcal disease, HPV, and influenza. A first meningococcal vaccine is recommended at age 11 or 12, with a booster dose at age 16 to protect the person through the college years. The HPV

The CDC distributes a variety of posters and pamphlets to promote immunization efforts in all age groups.

Older kids (adolescents, preteens, tweens, and teens) need vaccinations too, including Tdap, Meningococcal, HPV, and flu.

Ask your child's doctor or nurse if your child needs immunizations to protect against serious diseases.

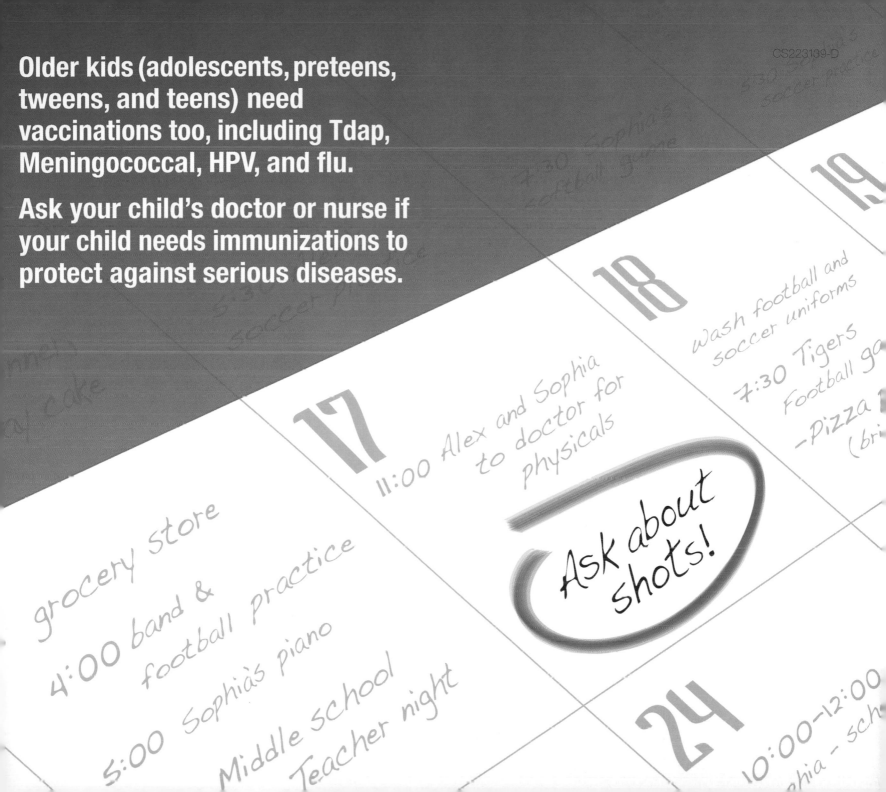

+ Combined Vaccines

Some vaccines can be combined into a single shot. Examples are the DTaP (diphtheria-tetanus-pertussis) and the MMR (measles-mumps-rubella) vaccines. Combining vaccines means fewer doctor visits, saving parents time and money. It is also less traumatic for the child, who receives fewer shots. Combined vaccines are just as effective as when given alone, and they show no more side effects.

vaccine is recommended for boys and girls at age 11 or 12. It protects against a virus that can cause a variety of cancers, most notably cervical cancer in women.

A few vaccines are also recommended for adults. Pneumococcal vaccine protects against the bacterium *Streptococcus pneumoniae*, which causes meningitis, pneumonia, and other diseases. It is given to high-risk groups, such as smokers, the elderly, and those with weakened immune systems or chronic illnesses. Finally, certain vaccines are recommended for people traveling internationally. These include vaccines for yellow fever, typhoid, rabies, and Japanese encephalitis.

Vaccine Side Effects

Vaccines do have side effects, called adverse events. Most are minor, and they can include redness, swelling, and soreness at the injection site. Some vaccines cause fever, rash, and aches. Very rarely, severe adverse events, or SAEs, occur. These may include seizures or life-threatening allergic reactions.

The type and severity of adverse events varies according to the type of vaccine given. For example, the Hib vaccine has few side effects. One of every four children shows heat, redness, and swelling at the infection site; one of every 20 children suffers a fever greater than 101 degrees Fahrenheit (38.3°C).[3] The smallpox vaccine is rarely used since smallpox was declared eradicated. Its side effects, in contrast to Hib, can be moderate to severe.

The variety of vaccines has expanded greatly in the past half century. Vaccine safety has also improved dramatically. Vaccine safety is closely monitored by the Vaccine Adverse Event Reporting System (VAERS), established in 1990 by the Centers for Disease Control and Prevention (CDC) and the Food and Drug Administration (FDA). But there is still much to learn about how to formulate vaccines, how to determine correct dosages, and how and when to administer them. In addition, scientists continue to make progress in understanding how both the immune system and vaccines work.

Vaccines and Public Health

The field of public health improves health and protects lives around the world. Individual countries have their own public health programs, such as the CDC in the United States. But infectious diseases do not stop at national borders. The most effective public health programs are often conducted by international organizations coordinating activities in many countries at once. They involve government groups and various nongovernmental organizations (NGOs).

Elimination versus Eradication

A major goal of worldwide public health programs is to eliminate or eradicate infectious diseases. Elimination means a disease is no longer spreading in a given region. For example, polio was declared eliminated in the Americas on September 29, 1994, and in Europe on June 21, 2002. Eradication

Workers for public health programs in India often deliver vaccine shipments to remote villages by bicycle.

International Public Health Programs

Agency/Program	Type	Function
Expanded Program on Immunization (EPI)	Part of UN World Health Organization (WHO)	Partners with countries and United Nations Children's Fund (UNICEF) to immunize children in all developing countries
GAVI Alliance (formerly Global Alliance for Vaccines and Immunization)	Diverse group of public and private stakeholders	Supports world's 72 poorest countries to increase childhood immunizations and introduce new technology
Global Immunization Division (GID)	Part of US CDC	Provides research and technical support to ministries of health and NGOs to control vaccine-preventable diseases worldwide
Bill & Melinda Gates Foundation	Private NGO	Supplies funding for Decade of Vaccines initiative of CDC's GID
Rotary International	Private NGO	Works on global eradication of polio through immunization
American Red Cross	Private NGO	Leads Measles & Rubella Initiative to reduce deaths through immunization

means worldwide elimination of a disease. So far, only one human disease—smallpox—has been eradicated. Smallpox was a good candidate for eradication for several reasons. First, it has an obvious red rash that appears shortly after exposure, so it cannot spread far without being noticed. Second, it is spread only by humans, not by other animals, which makes it easier to control. And third, either vaccination or surviving the disease gives a person lifelong immunity.

Other major diseases targeted by public health programs include Guinea worm disease, malaria, measles, mumps, and polio. Malaria is transmitted by mosquitoes, which are difficult to control. Additionally, having had malaria once does not result in lifelong immunity. People can get it repeatedly.

Because they spread malaria to millions of people every year, some scientists refer to mosquitoes as the world's deadliest animals.

Some diseases present other challenges that make them difficult to eliminate or eradicate. Polio often does not show symptoms, but a person lacking symptoms can still transmit it. Measles gives the sufferer an obvious rash, but carriers become infectious long before the rash appears. They can spread the disease without people realizing it.

Progress in the United States

The United States made great strides in the 1900s in immunizing children. By 1990, childhood vaccination was universally recommended for nine infectious diseases. By century's end, reported cases of these diseases had declined dramatically. Several new vaccines, including chicken pox and rotavirus, were introduced in the 1990s. They, too, proved extremely effective in radically reducing the number of cases.

But in the United States, approximately 42,000 adults and 300 children per year still die from vaccine-preventable diseases.[1] Several infectious diseases, including viral hepatitis, influenza, and tuberculosis, are still among the leading causes of illness and death. Every year, thousands of people in the United States die of influenza. Yet during the 2011–2012 flu season, only approximately 42 percent of Americans received the flu vaccine. CDC officials estimate these vaccinations prevented 5 million cases of flu and 40,000 hospitalizations.[2]

The Impact of Vaccines in the United States

Disease	Annual Reported Cases 1900	Annual Reported Cases 1998	Percent Decrease*
Smallpox	48,164	0	100
Diphtheria	175,885	1	100
Pertussis	147,271	6,279	95.7
Tetanus	1,314	34	97.4
Poliomyelitis (paralytic)	16,316	0	100
Measles	503,282	89	100
Mumps	152,209	606	99.6
Rubella	47,745	345	99.3
Haemophilus influenzae type B	20,000	54	99.7[5]

*Percentages rounded to nearest tenth

In 2010, US vaccination coverage for two-year-old children was approximately 80 percent for DTaP, 93 percent for polio and Hib, and 90 percent for MMR.[3] Although these statistics show parents are careful to vaccinate their young children, teens and adults are less protected. Only approximately half of all teens were vaccinated for meningococcal disease, and only 32 percent of girls received the complete series of vaccinations for HPV.[4] Both diseases can be deadly.

Even outbreaks of eliminated diseases still occur when vaccination rates drop. The United States still has periodic measles outbreaks. Pennsylvania and Minnesota suffered small outbreaks of Hib in 2008.

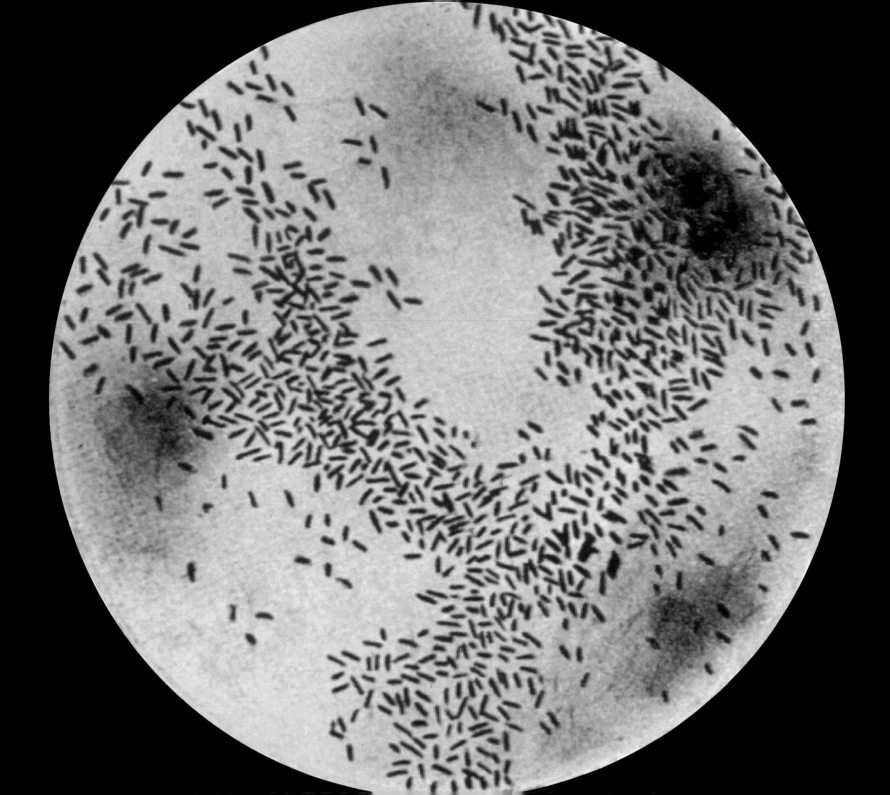

Only half of the affected children were vaccinated, and several children died. Perhaps most alarming, the CDC reported a 418 percent increase in cases of pertussis in California during the first half of 2010.[6] Most cases were in infants less than six months old, too young to be fully immunized. It is important, even in developed countries, to be vigilant about keeping vaccinations of both children and adults up-to-date.

Progress in the Developing World

The major causes of death in developing countries are infectious diseases. These include tuberculosis, measles, lower respiratory diseases, HIV/AIDS, and tropical diseases such as malaria. Developing countries are often poor and their residents have limited access to health care. More than 2 million children under age five still die annually

Has Measles Been Eliminated in the United States?

From 1989 to 1991, low immunization rates led to measles outbreaks across the United States, sickening 55,000 people and killing 123.[7] But in 2000, measles was declared eliminated. Has measles completely disappeared? Unfortunately, it has not. Not everyone is vaccinated, and measles is still brought in from other countries. Every year, approximately 60 cases of measles are reported in the United States. In 2011, this number rose to 222, with 17 separate outbreaks around the country. Nearly 40 percent of these people contracted the disease in foreign countries and brought it back to the United States.[8]

Hib, or *Haemophilus influenzae*, received its name during a flu pandemic when scientists mistakenly believed it caused influenza.

The Bill & Melinda Gates Foundation donated $750 million to establish GAVI. Since then the foundation has donated a total of $2.5 billion to the organization. [11]

from vaccine-preventable diseases. Millions more are permanently disabled.[9]

But immunization rates are rising. In 1974, when the WHO launched the Expanded Programme on Immunization (EPI), it targeted six diseases: diphtheria, pertussis, tetanus, measles, polio, and tuberculosis. At that time, fewer than 5 percent of children had been immunized against these diseases. Today, the immunization rate for one-year-olds is approximately 80 percent.[10] In addition, three new diseases are now being targeted—hepatitis B, Hib, and yellow fever. The Global Alliance for Vaccines and Immunization (GAVI), launched in 2000, stimulated the process. It made a commitment to increase the percentage of children immunized in the world's poorest countries. Originally, it took 15 to 20 years from the time a vaccine was approved in developed countries until it became available in the developing world. The wait time is now much shorter.

The impact of increased immunization rates around the world is dramatic. The lives of at least
20 million children have been saved in the past 20 years. Polio has been 99 percent eradicated and will
likely become the second disease ever to be fully eradicated. Measles deaths in Africa have decreased
by more than 90 percent in the last decade. Severe diarrhea due to rotavirus declined by 60 percent in

Nicaragua in the four years after rotavirus vaccine was introduced. Recently introduced vaccines for meningitis, pneumonia, cholera, and Japanese encephalitis will likely save the lives of hundreds of thousands of children per year.[12]

Future Prospects for Vaccines and Public Health

New procedures and technologies are improving world immunization programs, and new funding programs are stimulating development of vaccines specifically designed for diseases in developing countries. These include a malaria vaccine and a more effective vaccine against meningococcal meningitis. GAVI is introducing a vaccine that immunizes against five diseases at once: diphtheria, hepatitis B, Hib, pertussis, and tetanus. Children will need fewer shots and are more likely to receive all necessary vaccinations. Also, fewer vials of vaccine will need to be transported and kept in cold storage. This decreases the likelihood of vaccine damage. One innovation that improves the safety of vaccines is the auto-disable syringe. These types of syringes prevent reuse.

"Vaccines are a miracle because with three doses, mostly given in the first two years of life, you can prevent deadly diseases for an entire lifetime."[13]

—Bill Gates, Bill & Melinda Gates Foundation

When syringes are reused, often in an attempt to save money, there is a risk of transmitting a disease between the syringe users. By preventing reuse, auto-disable syringes help prevent the further spread of disease. Another important innovation is the temperature-sensitive label. Scientists and doctors can use these to determine whether a vaccine has been damaged by heat exposure.

Honduras: A Shot at Life

Honduras is the second-poorest country in Latin America. In the Western Hemisphere it ranks near the bottom in measures of literacy, education, life expectancy, and living standards. In 2000, Honduras also had high levels of infectious disease. But by 2012, more than 98 percent of Honduran children were vaccinated against preventable diseases. The cooperation of the United States, the Pan American Health Organization, and GAVI made this possible. Mumps decreased by 80 percent, measles by 74 percent, and tuberculosis by 43 percent.[14] Measles outbreaks were virtually eliminated.

6

The Process of Immunization

Getting a vaccine from the laboratory to the people who need it is a long, complex process. It begins with 10 to 15 years of laboratory research, field trials, and approvals by multiple agencies. Then, laboratories are geared up for large-scale production, which is monitored to ensure safety and quality. The final vaccine is stored and distributed under carefully controlled conditions. Procedures and regulations to ensure vaccine safety throughout this process were developed and standardized during the 1900s.

Development

Vaccine development begins when scientists and medical experts investigate a disease organism. They first isolate the bacterium or virus and study how it causes a disease. For example, is the disease

Many years and hundreds of millions of dollars are needed to take a vaccine from a scientific hypothesis to a mass-produced reality.

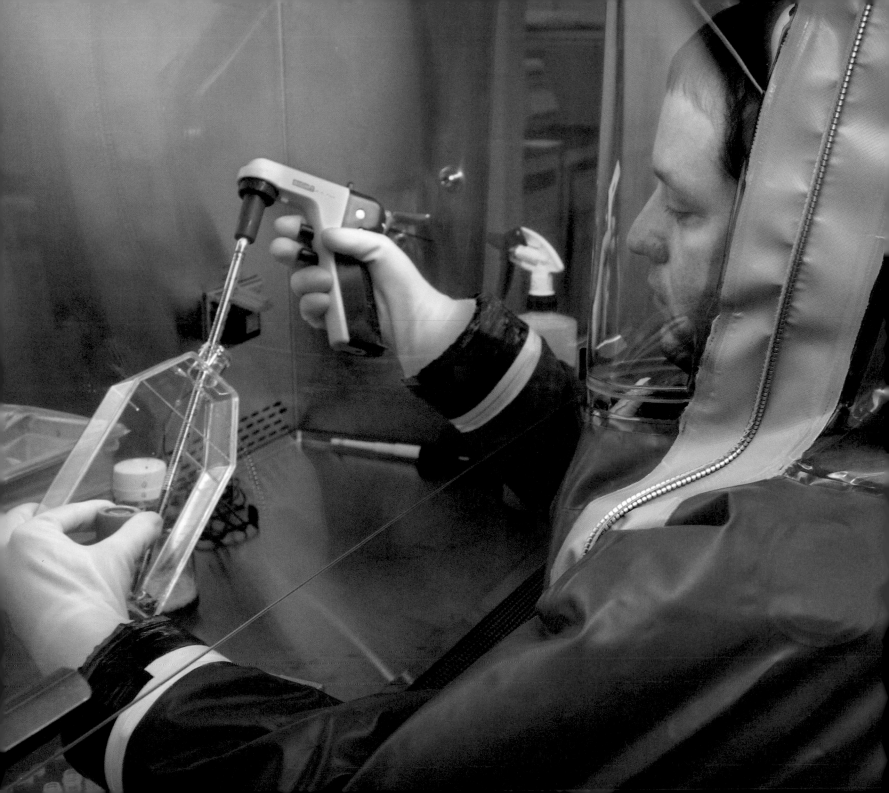

caused by the whole organism or by a toxin it produces? This information helps determine which type of vaccine will be needed. Researchers identify natural or synthetic antigens that could be used to make a vaccine. This exploratory stage of development usually lasts two to four years. It involves scientists from universities or governmental agencies. In the United States it is usually funded by the National Institutes of Health (NIH).

In the next stage, known as the preclinical stage, researchers spend up to two years studying the potential vaccine. To do so they use cell cultures and laboratory animals such as mice and monkeys. They determine the vaccine's ability to cause an immune response. They also obtain information on its safety and the likely dosage needed. They may also do "challenge" studies with laboratory animals. With this kind of study, scientists infect vaccinated animals with the pathogen and determine whether they get the disease. This process is done only in animals, never in humans. If the vaccine fails to produce a good immune response, research is discontinued.

If the vaccine seems to be a good candidate, the industry submits an application to the FDA for an Investigational New Drug (IND). The application describes both the research that has already been done and the proposed future research on the vaccine. A committee must review and approve the application. If approved, the vaccine enters three phases of clinical trials.

 Researchers must take extreme safety precautions when working with potentially deadly viruses.

Clinical Trials

Clinical trials with human subjects are highly regulated, with the regulation tightening as the vaccine progresses through the three phases. Studies in later phases are based on results of earlier ones. At any phase, if results show problems with either safety or effectiveness, trials can be stopped and the vaccine abandoned. Clinical trials are usually done by pharmaceutical companies.

Phase I trials are conducted on small groups of 20 to 80 healthy adult subjects. The trials may be nonblinded. That means researchers and possibly subjects know whether they are receiving the vaccine or a placebo. A placebo is a harmless substance that has no effect. It is used as a comparison to see whether the vaccine works. If the vaccine is meant for children, tests are first done on adults. The age of tests subjects is decreased over time until the target age is reached.

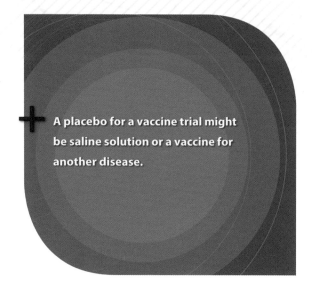

A placebo for a vaccine trial might be saline solution or a vaccine for another disease.

Phase II trials are conducted on several hundred people, including groups at risk for the disease. The vaccine is studied for safety, level of immune response, dosages, immunization schedule, and

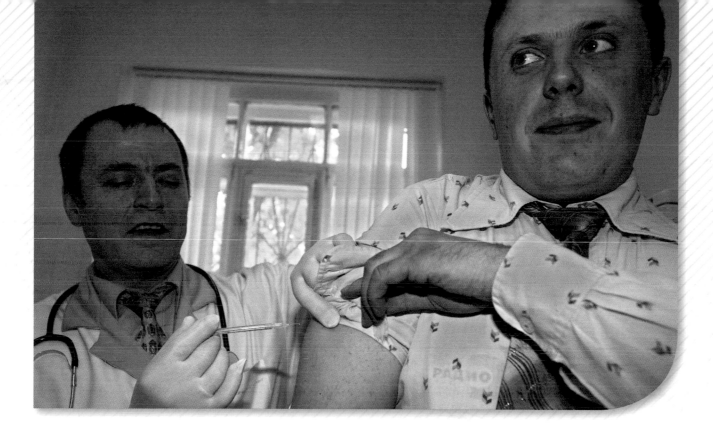

methods of delivery. In Phase II studies, it is random which subjects receive the vaccine and which the placebo.

Phase III trials involve at least 5,000 people and often tens of thousands. They are highly controlled, randomized, and double-blind. That means neither researchers nor subjects know who is receiving the vaccine and who is receiving the placebo. Phase III trials are conducted over a large geographic area. This is done to verify that people of different backgrounds and lifestyles react equally well to the

Making Flu Vaccines

Most new vaccines take years of development and testing before approval, but a new influenza vaccine is released every year. How is this possible? The manufacturing process and most ingredients in each year's vaccine remain the same. The only change is in the combination of antigens. Scientists continually track the influenza viruses present around the world. Each year they choose the three most likely to cause flu during the coming season. These antigens are included in that year's vaccine.

vaccine. The large, varied test population also helps determine safety. Rare side effects that did not occur in smaller, healthy populations may become evident in Phase III trials.

Approval and Licensing

After a vaccine passes all three phases of clinical trials, it is still not ready to be given to the public. Data from the trials go through an intensive review process. First, the developer submits an application to the FDA. The FDA checks the data to make sure the trials were done correctly and the results are consistent. They also inspect the factory where the vaccine will be made and approve the wording of its label. They will continue to monitor the vaccine production process, the facilities, and samples of the vaccine throughout its production.

After FDA approval, the study information is sent to the Advisory Committee on Immunization Practices (ACIP).

This group of scientists and doctors advises the CDC. They recommend how and by whom the vaccine should be used. The CDC, the American Academy of Pediatrics, and the American Academy of Family Physicians together make a final recommendation. Doctors use this recommendation to determine who should receive the new vaccine.

Production

Finally, the new vaccine is ready to be administered to millions of people around the world. It is ready for large-scale factory production, which involves three stages. These are generation of the antigen, purification, and formulation.

To generate the antigen, the pathogen must first be produced and grown. Different pathogens are made using different methods. Viruses are grown in cells such as chicken eggs, in cell lines, or in cultured human cells. Bacterial pathogens, such as Hib, are usually grown in large bioreactors. A bioreactor is a chamber filled with nutrients and maintained under conditions that allow bacteria to grow. For live, attenuated vaccines, weakening of the pathogen with heat or chemicals also occurs during this phase.

After the antigen is produced, it must be purified. Attenuated viruses usually require no further purification, but other types require additional purification procedures. Finally, extra ingredients are added to complete the vaccine. These include adjuvants, stabilizers, and preservatives. Adjuvants aid or

enhance the immune response. Stabilizers make it possible to store the vaccine for long periods of time.
Preservatives allow doctors to get multiple doses out of a single vial of vaccine without spoiling it.

The Cold Chain

After the vaccine is produced, it often must be delivered to faraway clinics. Because most vaccines must
be kept at specific temperatures, this transportation must be done very carefully. Going above or below

Most vaccines must be kept at temperatures between 35 and 46 degrees Fahrenheit (2 and 8°C).

these temperature limits can damage a vaccine, making it less effective. A system of procedures and equipment called the cold chain is used to keep the vaccine within this temperature range from the time it is produced until it is given to a patient.

The CDC has developed guidelines for making sure vaccines do not get too hot or too cold. These include the careful selection of refrigerators or cold boxes at every step of the transport process, constant temperature monitoring and documentation, and immediate reaction if the temperature increases or decreases too much. The United Nations Children's Fund operates the Cold Chain and Logistics system, which provides guidelines for maintaining a cold chain during distribution. These guidelines work even when delivering to hard-to-reach clinics in developing countries.

Vaccines with Special Temperature Needs

Two recently introduced vaccines—the chicken pox vaccine and the live, attenuated influenza vaccine (LAIV)—have different temperature requirements than most. They must remain frozen at temperatures of five degrees Fahrenheit (-15°C) or less.[1] Freezing, thawing, and refreezing can be damaging to them. Because of this, when scientists transport them along with other vaccines, they need a separate freezer.

Adjuvants and Safety

Only two types of adjuvants, aluminum salt and gel-based, are currently licensed for use in the United States. Other types cause a stronger immune response but are also more toxic, so they are no longer used. Several new, stronger adjuvants have been developed and are currently undergoing clinical tests. A few of these have already been approved by other countries.

Phase IV Trials

Clinical trials do not stop after the vaccine is licensed and distributed. Once the vaccine is being used, Phase IV trials monitor the effectiveness and safety of the vaccine in the real world. In the United States, the CDC carries out trials in cooperation with local health departments. Health departments monitor people receiving the vaccine and report the numbers to the CDC. Also, the CDC keeps track of occurrences of the disease and compares them with vaccination schedules.

Vaccine safety is also monitored by VAERS. VAERS monitors adverse events and identifies possible patient risk factors. Doctors and hospitals report any adverse events they notice in their patients. The organization also identifies vaccine batches associated with adverse events and assesses the safety of newly released vaccines. Another safety organization, the Vaccine Safety Datalink (VSD), is a cooperative project between the CDC and hospital groups around the United States. The VSD gathers and shares data on vaccinations, medical outcomes, and birth and census data. This helps them plan investigations and determine any problems with vaccines currently in use.

In the past few decades, procedures for developing, producing, transporting, and monitoring vaccines have benefited from advances in medicine and technology. Recently, private organizations have provided an influx of money for vaccines. The Bill & Melinda Gates Foundation, for example, pledged $10 billion between 2010 and 2020. This money is intended to "help research, develop and deliver vaccines for the world's poorest countries."[2] The combination of money, new technologies, and the cooperation of committed groups aims to accelerate the eradication of infectious disease throughout the world.

7

The Anti-Vaccine Controversy

People have feared and opposed vaccination as long as it has existed. Anti-vaccination fervor in England began in earnest with objections to Jenner's cowpox vaccine. It reached a fever pitch in the late 1800s with the formation of anti-vaccination leagues. People had sanitary, religious, and political objections to vaccines. In 1879, the opposition reached the United States. Smallpox outbreaks led to vaccine campaigns and ultimately laws requiring vaccination. These in turn led to the formation of the Anti-Vaccination Society of America and several state and regional groups. In 1905, the US Supreme Court ruled that states had the right to require vaccination. But in both the United States and Europe, anti-vaccination controversies continue.

During a 2009 swine flu pandemic, protests broke out over the issue of vaccination against the disease.

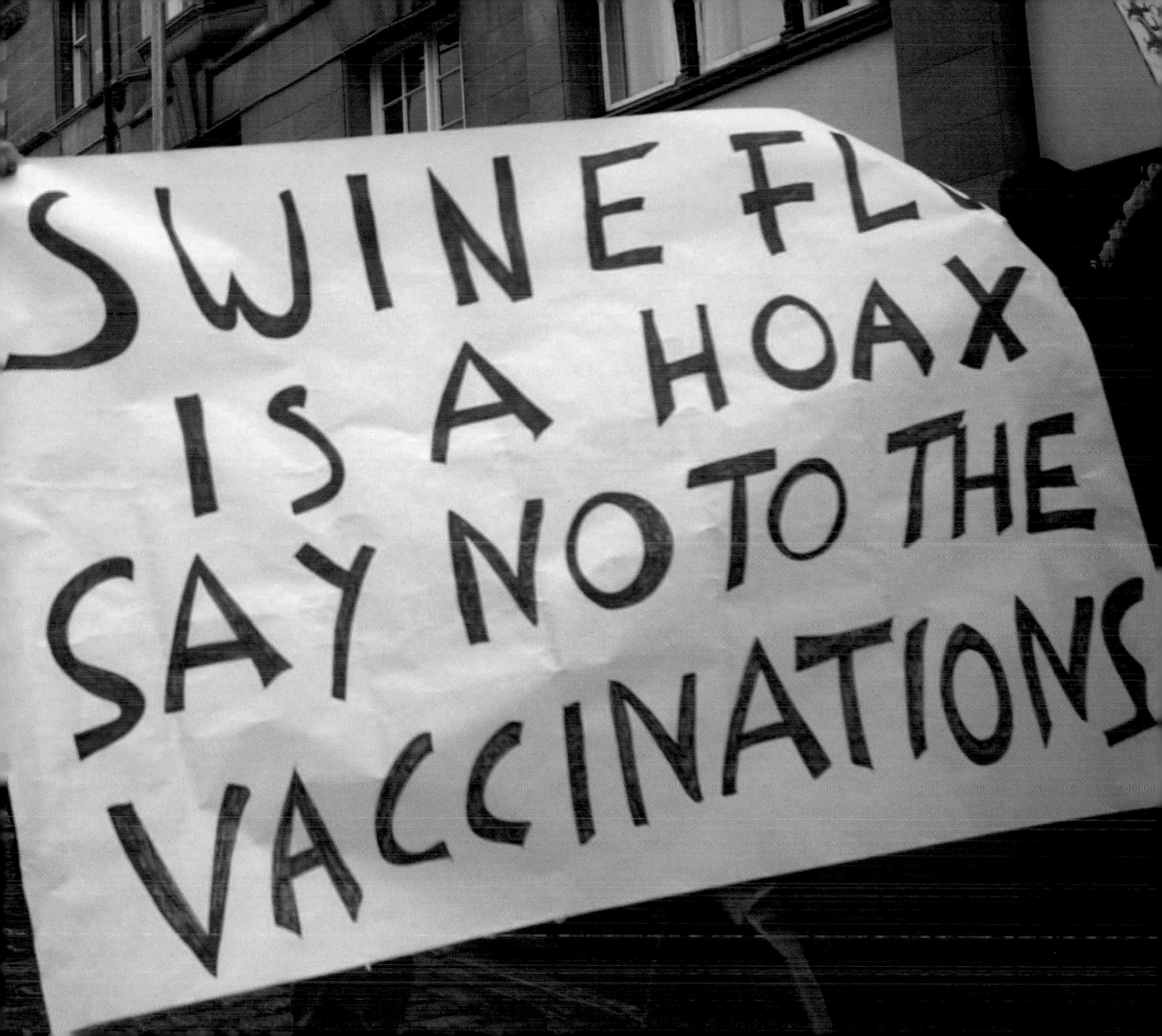
SWINE FL
IS A HOAX
SAY NO TO THE
VACCINATIONS

Leicester Protests Vaccination

The British town of Leicester showed its opposition to England's mandatory smallpox vaccination law with the Leicester Demonstration March of 1885. The march included 80,000 to 100,000 protesters and featured a child's coffin and an effigy of British scientist Edward Jenner.[2] In response to vaccine opposition, a commission was formed to study vaccination. It ruled that vaccination did protect against smallpox. It also recommended changing the law to remove penalties for non-vaccination and to include an exemption for those who objected. The law was amended in 1898.

Why People Fear Vaccines

An increasing number of American parents today either refuse to vaccinate their children or choose to delay or forgo some recommended vaccinations. Although some public health officials claim parents do this out of ignorance, more of these parents are college-educated than not. Educated parents want to take a more active role in protecting their children. In addition, particularly since the 1990s, there has been strong mainstream media coverage of anti-vaccination ideas. According to journalist Mark A. Largent, this coverage has convinced many people that vaccines are "unsafe, ineffective, untested, and overused."[1]

Many claims against vaccines began in the alternative medicine movement, including among chiropractors. Chiropractors adhere to "natural medicine," in which the body supposedly heals itself. Many have a religious or mystical, rather than scientific, approach to medicine.

Some chiropractors attribute decreased levels of disease not to vaccines but to better sanitation, better nutrition, and disease patterns throughout history. They also worry about side effects of vaccines. Some of these side effects are described in the medical literature, but others are based on media reports and not backed by evidence. Since the founding of chiropractic in the 1890s, the scientifically based American Medical Association (AMA), which licenses physicians, has opposed chiropractic methods.

Many assertions by alternative medical practitioners show a lack of scientific and medical understanding about vaccines. For example, an anti-vaccination chiropractor has said most modern vaccines "are made up of experimental proteins from rotting, diseased samples of animal tissue." He also says "there is no general agreement" that vaccination causes the body to produce antibodies that confer immunity, and "there is no convincing scientific evidence that mass inoculation can be credited with eliminating any infectious disease."[3] These statements are false.

Vaccine Safety and Side Effects

Some concerns about vaccine safety are valid. For example, some concerns are based on the ingredients used to make vaccines, such as cells and tissues originating from humans, cows, monkeys, chickens, and guinea pigs.

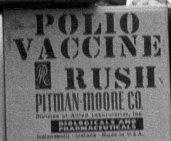

Between 1955 and 1963, monkey kidney cells used in both the Salk and Sabin vaccines were found to be contaminated with the SV-40 virus. This virus is known to trigger various cancers in humans. Nearly 30 million people were injected with these vaccines.[4] However, recent studies show cancer rates are no higher in the vaccinated group than in unvaccinated people. Also, a type of pig virus was found in rotavirus vaccine in 2010. This virus is harmless to humans and is unlikely to remain in the body long. Therefore, the vaccine is still used, although further studies are being done. Vaccines are now thoroughly tested for all known infectious diseases—bacterial and viral—before being released. They are now considered extremely safe.

The presence of aluminum adjuvants in vaccines also worries some people. Aluminum occurs naturally in the environment and has been considered harmless because such small amounts are ingested. But recently, people have become concerned about aluminum toxicity in babies. Because newborns receive so many vaccinations, some fear aluminum may build to toxic levels in their brains and bones. This is of particular concern for premature babies. The FDA has set a maximum level of aluminum allowable

Some scientists worry about possible undetected vaccine contaminants. These include very small viruses and agents called prions or slow viruses, which may slip through current testing procedures. So far, no problems have occurred from such contaminants.

The extent of the SV-40 contamination of some early vaccines was not fully understood until more than 40 years after their introduction.

in a single vaccine. But no studies have been done to validate the safety of this level. According to pediatrician Robert W. Sears, this is a neglected area of research.

Other chemicals are used in vaccines in very small amounts. Even though some are toxic in larger doses, doctors (including Sears) feel the tiny amounts used in vaccines render them harmless.

Recent Vaccine Controversies

In the 1970s, a controversy arose in the United Kingdom around the use of the combined DPT (diphtheria, pertussis, tetanus) vaccine. A London hospital reported that 36 children suffered from brain-related conditions following DPT vaccination.[5] Use of the DPT vaccine was suspended until independent studies confirmed its safety. Vaccination rates in the United Kingdom decreased, leading to multiple pertussis epidemics. In the United States, fear of the vaccine was spread by media attention, especially a 1982 documentary (*DPT: Vaccination Roulette*) and a 1991 book (*A Shot in the Dark*). Medical groups including the Academy of Pediatrics and the CDC rebutted these claims, and vaccination rates in the United States were not seriously affected.

The original DPT vaccine had more side effects than most vaccines, including irritability, high fever, and occasional fever-related seizures. These resulted from the whole-cell pertussis vaccine, which has now been replaced with a new, safer form of the vaccine. The original DPT vaccine was also blamed for

Pertussis outbreaks have returned to the United States where vaccination rates have fallen. A 2010 outbreak in California resulted in the deaths of several infants.

AIDS, Vaccines, and the Media

By the early 1980s, medical researchers had determined that acquired immunodeficiency syndrome (AIDS) was caused by human immunodeficiency virus (HIV). Evidence suggested it entered humans in the early 1900s, probably when a person ate or was bitten by an infected chimpanzee. This was known as the natural transfer hypothesis. In the 1980s and 1990s, a competing hypothesis arose—the OPV HIV hypothesis. According to this idea, HIV entered humans in the 1950s through a contaminated oral polio vaccine used in the Belgian Congo. Although HIV entered humans approximately two decades before the polio vaccine existed, some polio vaccines were contaminated with monkey viruses, making the story sound plausible to some. This story shows how strongly the public can be influenced by media reports. But it also drew attention to lax standards in vaccine production. This in turn led to tightened regulations that have resulted in much safer vaccines.

reports of sudden infant death syndrome and onset of some chronic diseases. These reports are now known to be untrue.

In 1998, British physician Andrew Wakefield and 12 colleagues published a case study in the medical journal the *Lancet*. The case study describes 12 children who developed intestinal problems and signs of autism shortly after receiving the MMR vaccine. The paper concludes the vaccine was responsible. Resulting public fears caused a drop in vaccination rates, and measles outbreaks followed. Ten of the twelve coauthors later rejected the study's conclusion. Dr. Wakefield was shown to have a conflict of interest and to have tampered with the data. The validity of the study has been completely dispelled and it has been fully retracted by the *Lancet*. British parents did see a correlation with the increase in autism and the introduction of the MMR vaccine in 1987. But the MMR vaccine had been used in the United States since 1971, long before a rise in autism was noticed.

A second hypothesis concerning vaccines and autism began in the United States. It linked autism to the vaccine preservative thimerosal. This organic compound containing mercury has been added to vaccines to prevent bacterial contamination since the 1930s. It has proven both safe and effective. However, to ensure babies taking many vaccines do not receive excessive doses of mercury, thimerosal was removed from infant vaccines between 1999 and 2001. A 2008 California study showed elimination of thimerosal has not affected the rise of autism. Two reports by the Institute of Medicine's Immunization Safety Review Committee found no indication thimerosal causes autism or other disorders. But anti-vaccination groups such as Generation Rescue and Talk About Curing Autism still believe thimerosal is dangerous. They promote a "Green Our Vaccines" campaign to remove what they believe are toxins from vaccines.

In contrast, another incident highlighted the medical community's ability to respond to real problems with vaccines. RotaShield, the first rotavirus vaccine, caused a slight risk of intussusception, a bowel blockage that sometimes requires surgery. This vaccine was quickly removed and replaced with two new vaccines. The new vaccines underwent thorough testing and were found to be safe. According to pediatrician Daniel R. Bronfin, the immediate withdrawal of the vaccine and rigorous testing of

its replacements is evidence of the United States' dedication to vaccine safety.

Vaccines are not perfect. Neither is the system of developing and testing them. But in the last half century, rapid advances in methods of developing vaccines and monitoring and testing safety have greatly decreased the number of side effects. Vaccines are safer than ever before. Many parents are still concerned about the large number of vaccines now recommended for very small children. Some have concerns about specific vaccines. Medical professionals, including pediatricians, the CDC, and the FDA, provide detailed information on all vaccines. Thus, parents can choose whether to give their children all recommended vaccines or to skip a vaccine about which they have concerns. But medical groups strongly advocate following the complete vaccination schedule. On one of its Web sites for public information, the US government outlines its position: "Vaccinating your child is one of the most important steps you can take to protect their health and future."[6]

> Many celebrities, such as actress and model Jenny McCarthy, have accused vaccinations of causing autism. They have many followers, even though scientists have refuted their claims.

Actress and model Jenny McCarthy, *right*, has been a vocal opponent of vaccines, claiming they caused autism in her son.

8

Vaccines of Tomorrow

In the coming decades, immunologists and public health workers will be busy in several areas. Research will concentrate on increasing knowledge of vaccine and immune system mechanisms. Additionally, it will focus on developing new vaccines and technologies for improving vaccines. Efforts are also under way to develop vaccines that prevent noninfectious, chronic diseases. These diseases, such as cancer and heart disease, generally last a long time and develop slowly. Public health programs to deliver vaccines to remote areas will continue and expand. New, innovative programs are being tried to further these efforts. Finally, a less-publicized but vital goal of public health and immunology research is dealing with bioterrorism. In other words, if a terrorist unleashes a biological weapon, such as a disease-causing virus, who will respond, and how? Meeting these challenges will not be easy.

Because of extremely long lead times, work is only just beginning on vaccines that will save lives decades from now.

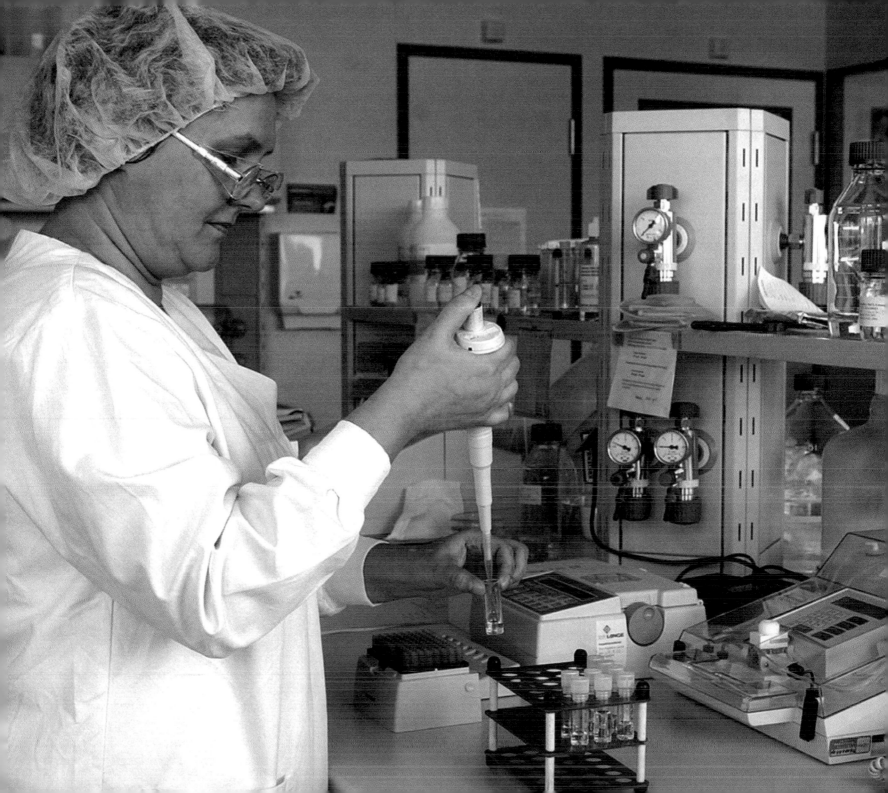

Future Vaccines

Pathologist G. J. Nossal gives this possible timeline for when new vaccines will become available to the public.

Disease	Likely Time of Availability (years)
Typhoid fever	0–10
Shigellosis (a type of dysentery)	0–10
Neisseria meningitidis (causes meningitis)	0–10
Streptococcus pneumoniae (causes pneumonia and other diseases)	0–10
Malaria	0–19
Tuberculosis	10–19
HIV/AIDS	10–19
Vaccines for autoimmune diseases (juvenile diabetes, celiac disease)	20–50[1]

New Vaccines and Vaccine Technologies

According to pathologist G. J. Nossal, we can probably expect new vaccines for several infectious diseases in the next ten years. These vaccines will be similar in form and production to currently available ones. Within 20 years, there may be new vaccines for the diseases Nossal calls the "big three"—malaria, tuberculosis, and HIV/AIDS. The vaccine for malaria is closest to completion. However, fully preventing malaria will most likely require a vaccine containing several antigens. Each antigen would attack a different stage of the parasite's life cycle. An effective tuberculosis vaccine will also require several antigens. In the long term, in 20 to 50 years, vaccines will likely become available for chronic diseases. Good candidates for vaccines include autoimmune diseases such as juvenile diabetes and celiac

disease. For these types of vaccines, researchers hope to find a way to correct the problems with a patient's immune system.

Some future vaccines will employ live organisms. In this type of vaccine, one type of pathogen is injected to protect against a disease caused by a different type. A few vaccines already use this method, such as the hepatitis B vaccine. This technique is used either to enhance the immune response or because using the disease-causing organism itself is too dangerous. This is the case with HIV. If it is given whole in a vaccine, a person could contract the virus. Another future trend is the therapeutic vaccine. Some of these drugs work by instructing the immune system on how to effectively fight pathogens.

Therapeutic vaccines provide hope for chronic noninfectious diseases, such as Alzheimer's disease, which causes degeneration of nervous tissue. Some are also being tested for use against AIDS, to be used alongside standard drugs.

Many future vaccines will be based on methods of enhancing the immune response. Three current approaches include development of new adjuvants, prime-boost strategies, and mucosal immunity. Prime-boost strategies use two vaccines to help each other be more effective in preventing disease. Mucosal immunity is the ability of the body's mucous membranes—such as the surface of the respiratory tract—to fight pathogens. Along with the skin itself, these locations are the body's first line of defense against pathogens.

A promising type of vaccine is the deoxyribonucleic acid (DNA) vaccine, which contains a piece of DNA coding for an antigen. DNA is the substance within an organism's cells that contains coded information about the organism and how it is made. The DNA vaccine is directly injected into the muscle. Like the person's own DNA, it directs production of a protein—in this case, the antigen for a disease. When the protein generates an immune response, it causes production of antibodies against the disease. DNA vaccines are exciting because they are stable and easy to manufacture. They may eventually be used against parasitic diseases such as malaria, for which no vaccines currently exist. But so far, no DNA vaccine has shown a strong enough immune response to prevent infection.

Seeking an HIV Vaccine

HIV attacks a type of T cells called helper T cells, destroying the body's ability to fight other infections. When blood helper T cell levels decrease below a certain point, the person has progressed from HIV infection to AIDS. Vaccine development is difficult because the AIDS virus mutates rapidly. A vaccine that works against one form of the virus may not work against others. A few individuals' bodies are capable of naturally regulating their HIV levels, preventing the disease from progressing to AIDS. Researchers hope to find clues for better vaccines by studying these people.

The largest and most promising trial of an HIV vaccine was completed in 2009. This six-year effort studied more than 16,000 people in Thailand.[2] The trial vaccine, called RV144, used a prime-boost strategy. It contained two vaccines: a prime vaccine based on a canary pox virus, and a boost vaccine made from a genetically engineered protein from HIV. The prime was intended to stimulate T cells to destroy infected cells. The boost was meant to stimulate B cells to make antibodies against HIV. The trial showed 31 percent fewer HIV cases with the vaccine than with the placebo.[3] This is not a strong enough response for a final vaccine, but the results are encouraging. Scientists will continue to study how the vaccine works and how to improve it.

New Public Health Technologies

Although great strides have been made in public health by the distribution of vaccines, much remains to be done. Immunization programs cannot just immunize everyone once. The program must be sustained year after year to provide continuing immunity. This is difficult even in developed countries. It is worse in poor countries where immunization rates are still low and many areas are hard to reach. Also, all aspects of an immunization program—from vaccine development to manufacture and storage through distribution—are very expensive. They require strong cooperation among many groups plus creative financing strategies.

One of the easiest ways to promote vaccination and to increase vaccination rates is simply for public officials to lead by example.

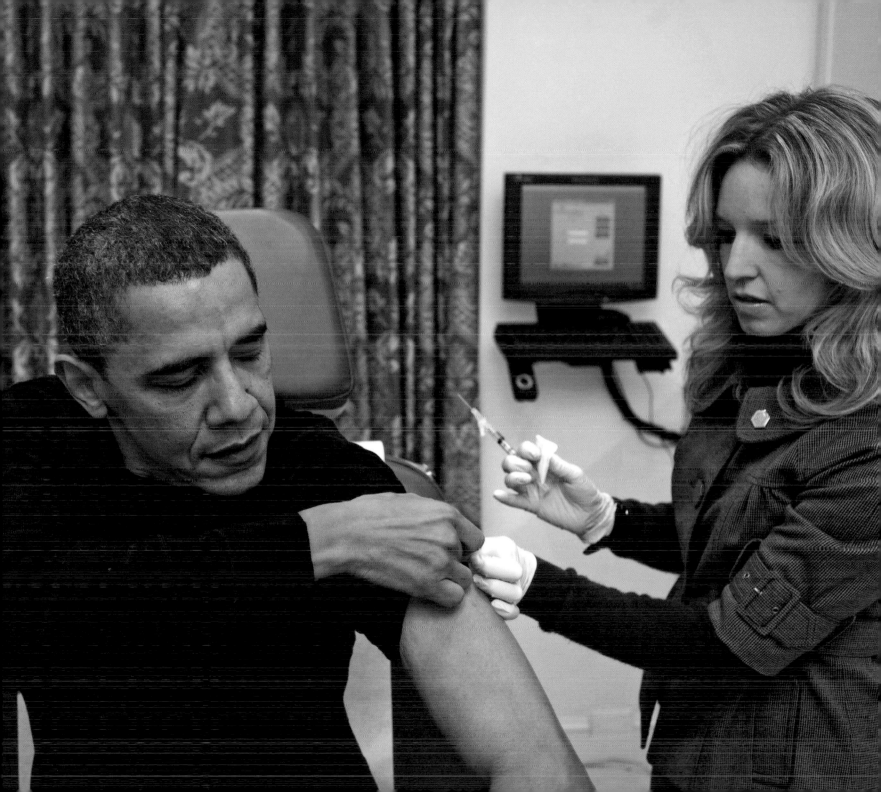

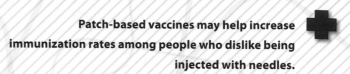
One factor that could assist the distribution of vaccines in both developed and developing countries is a change in delivery methods. Many vaccines today are delivered by injection. Shots must be given by trained personnel who are often not available in developing areas. In the future, vaccines may be inhaled or absorbed through a patch. An inhaled vaccine is already used to deliver some influenza vaccines. In patch delivery, a patch containing a pattern of very tiny needles delivers the vaccine without use of a syringe.

The cold chain system for storing and delivering vaccines also needs improvement. Refrigeration facilities are often not available in developing countries where vaccines are most needed. A new method of transporting the vaccine could solve this problem. Instead of liquid vaccine stored in vials, researchers have tried coating a very thin filter-like membrane with an even thinner layer of glass. The vaccine is then trapped between the two layers. In this form, vaccines withstood temperatures up to 113 degrees Fahrenheit (45°C) for six months without losing potency. In liquid form, one out of every two vaccines tested was destroyed in a week.[4] The researchers also tested a method of attaching the trapped virus particles to a fluid-filled syringe. This allowed the vaccine to be mixed and injected almost simultaneously. Although still under testing, this is a promising new method.

Tackling Bioterrorism

Bioterrorism is the deliberate release of bacteria or viruses that cause disease. Bioterrorists intend to frighten people or incapacitate a population by causing disease outbreaks or epidemics. The weapons used in bioterrorism vary. Potentially deadly agents (Category A) include anthrax, smallpox, and Ebola viruses. Other agents (Categories B and C) are less deadly, but easier to spread.

How likely is a biological attack in the United States? Some consider it more likely than a nuclear attack. Others disagree because it is difficult to weaponize and release biological agents in large

TIME
HOW REAL IS THE THREAT?
Germ and chemical warfare.
Suicide bombers. Nuclear weapons.
A jittery nation needs to
separate REALITY from RUMOR.
Here are the facts.
PLUS: The Hunt for Bin Laden

quantities. Two such attacks have already occurred. In 1984, members of an Oregon cult introduced salmonella bacteria into local food supplies, causing nearly 800 illnesses but no deaths.[5] In 2001, shortly after the September 11 attacks on the World Trade Center and the Pentagon, another attack occurred. An unknown person mailed letters contaminated with the dangerous disease anthrax to two US senators and several media groups. Anthrax can attack the respiratory system or the digestive system, depending on how it enters the body. Seventeen people became ill, and five died.[6]

A major challenge in responding to bioterrorist threats is the need for a vaccine to counteract every potential biological weapon. Currently, large quantities of vaccine are available only for smallpox and anthrax. Enough smallpox vaccine has been stockpiled to vaccinate the entire country. The anthrax vaccine has been used by millions of military personnel but has not been tested in children. In 2011, tests on children were recommended, but some people objected. They felt children should not be exposed to the risks of testing based on such an unlikely event.

Some experts consider a bioterrorist attack very unlikely but believe preparing for one will also improve responses to other types of health emergencies.

Bioterrorism entered the American public consciousness in a dramatic fashion after the 2001 anthrax attacks.

America's Disease Detectives

One way the United States cooperates in the public health field is through its "disease detectives." These members of the Epidemic Intelligence Service (EIS) are health professionals who tackle public health problems around the world. The CDC founded the EIS in 1951. Its workers investigate and assist in public health emergencies, including epidemics and other disasters. Some of the many situations they have responded to include:

1957: Asian flu pandemic originating in Hong Kong

1966: World smallpox eradication campaign

1976: Ebola virus outbreak in Zaire and Sudan

1984: Intentional salmonella poisoning in Oregon (first known US bioterrorist event)

1992: Hurricane Andrew

2001: Terrorist attack on the World Trade Center and anthrax attacks

2005: Hurricane Katrina

2009: H1N1 (swine flu) pandemic

A further complication is that some potential bioterrorist weapons do not exist in nature and could instead be created in laboratories. It is impossible to make a vaccine against an unknown agent. Given the 10- to 20-year lead time needed to develop a single vaccine, scientists must make educated guesses about which biological weapons will most likely be used. Finally, even if vaccines are developed, there still exists the challenge and expense of producing and maintaining a large enough stockpile of doses to counter a large attack.

The FDA, which licenses vaccines, has rapid pathways for licensing vaccines in case of emergencies. Licensing may be sped up if a vaccine has shown clear therapeutic value, even if testing is not completed. In more drastic situations, animal studies alone, rather than full clinical trials, might be sufficient for approval. The US Strategic National Stockpile contains smallpox and anthrax vaccines, other vaccines, antiviral drugs, and medical supplies. Some vaccines provide immunity if given immediately after exposure, but others must be given in advance. For several diseases, such as tularemia, anthrax, and plague, antibodies could be directly injected into a person to provide immediate protection.

Vaccines already developed and administered around the world have done a spectacular job of saving lives by preventing infectious disease. Work is ongoing to increase immunization rates and provide long-term protection to people in areas not yet fully immunized, including Africa, Asia, and Latin America. In the 2000s, this work will continue with the addition of new vaccines and new methods of vaccine transport and delivery. Doctors and scientists around the world will continue to monitor and respond to emergencies. And behind the scenes, researchers will continue to learn more about the immune system. They will continue to provide the world with medical marvels in the form of vaccines to prevent both infectious and noninfectious chronic diseases in the next century.

✚ Timeline

1721

Variolation reaches England and North America.

1796

On May 14, Edward Jenner inoculates eight-year-old James Phipps with material from a cowpox sore, beginning his experiment on smallpox immunity.

1813

The US Congress passes a bill establishing the National Vaccine Agency.

1879

In France, Louis Pasteur produces the first laboratory-made vaccine, for chicken cholera.

1885

Pasteur prevents rabies in a nine-year-old boy using post-exposure vaccination.

1955

Jonas Salk's polio vaccine is licensed in the United States on April 12.

1955

The Cutter Incident occurs in late April, leading to the creation of standards to oversee vaccine safety and regulation.

1961

Albert Sabin's oral polio vaccine is licensed in the United States.

1974

The WHO launches the Expanded Programme on Immunization (EPI), targeting diphtheria, pertussis, tetanus, measles, polio, and tuberculosis.

1980

The WHO declares the world free from smallpox.

1897

Paul Ehrlich develops a standardized unit for measuring antitoxin.

1905

The US Supreme Court rules states have the right to require vaccination.

1916

The first major polio epidemic in the United States begins in the summer in New York City.

1936

Max Theiler creates a successful yellow fever vaccine.

1938

Franklin D. Roosevelt founds the March of Dimes, and Eddie Cantor publicizes it to fund the fight against polio.

1990

The Vaccine Adverse Event Reporting System (VAERS) is founded by the FDA and CDC.

1994

Polio is declared eliminated in the Americas on September 29.

2000

Measles is declared eliminated in the United States.

2002

Polio is declared eliminated in Europe on June 21.

2010

On January 29, the Bill & Melinda Gates Foundation pledges $10 billion over ten years to provide vaccines for the world's poorest countries.

✚ Glossary

acquired immunity

Immunity developed by exposure to a disease, either naturally or by vaccination.

adjuvant

A substance, such as aluminum, that improves the effectiveness of a vaccine.

adverse event

A side effect of a vaccine.

antibody

A special protein, also called an immunoglobulin, produced by the body to fight disease; each antibody targets a specific antigen.

antigen

A foreign substance that enters the body and stimulates the immune system to produce antibodies that target it.

antitoxin

An antibody that counteracts a toxin.

attenuated

Weakened.

cell culture

The growth of a cell in a laboratory rather than in an organism.

cell line

Identical cells grown from a single cell.

epidemic

An outbreak of disease in a particular area.

inoculation

The process of introducing organisms, infective material, or other substances into an organism to create immunity to a disease.

leukocyte

A white blood cell, part of the body's immune system, which is responsible for destroying disease organisms.

memory cell

A white blood cell that enables the body to remember antigens and stimulates antibody production when the antigen is next encountered.

natural immunity

The immunity present when a person is born.

pandemic

An outbreak of disease across an entire country or the world.

quarantined

Kept away from others to avoid spreading a disease.

therapeutic vaccine

A vaccine that stimulates the immune system to treat, rather than prevent, a viral infection.

toxoid

An inactivated bacterial toxin used in a vaccine.

Additional Resources

Selected Bibliography

Allen, Arthur. *Vaccine: The Controversial Story of Medicine's Greatest Lifesaver*. New York: Norton, 2007. Print.

Largent, Mark A. *Vaccine: The Debate in Modern America*. Baltimore, MD: Johns Hopkins UP, 2012. Print.

Mnookin, Seth. *The Panic Virus: A True Story of Medicine, Science, and Fear*. New York: Simon, 2011. Print.

Further Readings

Allman, Toney. *Vaccine Research (Inside Science)*. San Diego, CA: Referencepoint, 2010. Print.

Engdahl, Sylvia. *Vaccines (Current Controversies)*. Farmington Hills, MI: Greenhaven, 2008. Print.

Merino, Noël. *Vaccines (Introducing Issues with Opposing Viewpoints)*. Farmington Hills, MI: Greenhaven, 2012. Print.

Web Sites

To learn more about vaccines, visit ABDO Publishing Company online at **www.abdopublishing.com**. Web sites about vaccines are featured on our Book Links page. These links are routinely monitored and updated to provide the most current information available.

For More Information

Centers for Disease Control and Prevention (CDC)

1600 Clifton Road
Atlanta, GA 30333
800-232-4636
http://www.cdc.gov/vaccines

The CDC is the US government's major organization dedicated to problems of public health, disease, injury, and disability.

World Health Organization (WHO)

Avenue Appia 20
1211 Geneva 27, Switzerland
+ 41 22 791 21 11
http://www.who.int/topics/vaccines/en

The WHO is the United Nations organization responsible for leadership on global health, including immunization for infectious diseases. The Web site has general and specific information about vaccines plus descriptions of public health programs around the world.

Source Notes

Chapter 1. Polio: Scourge of Summer

1. "Communities." *Whatever Happened to Polio?* Smithsonian National Museum of American History, 2012. Web. 10 Apr. 2013.

2. Ibid.

3. "Polio." *Kids Health*. The Nemours Foundation, 2010. Web. 10 Apr. 2013.

4. Ibid.

5. Ibid.

6. "Incidence Rates of Poliomyelitis in US." *PHI*. PHI, n.d. Web. 10 Apr. 2013.

7. Arthur Allen. *Vaccine: The Controversial Story of America's Greatest Lifesaver*. New York: Norton, 2007. Print. 166.

8. Ibid. 186–188.

9. "Clinical Trials." *Whatever Happened to Polio?* Smithsonian National Museum of American History, 2012. Web. 10 Apr. 2013.

10. Arthur Allen. *Vaccine: The Controversial Story of America's Greatest Lifesaver*. New York: Norton, 2007. Print. 197–199.

11. Ibid. 208.

12. "Incidence Rates of Poliomyelitis in US." *PHI*. PHI, n.d. Web. 10 Apr. 2013.

13. Ibid.

14. "Immunization and Infectious Disease." *HealthyPeople.gov*. US Department of Health and Human Services, 6 Sept. 2012. Web. 10 Apr. 2013.

Chapter 2. Introducing Vaccines

1. "Achievements in Public Health, 1900–1999: Control of Infectious Diseases." *MMWR Weekly*. CDC, 30 July 1999. Web. 10 Apr. 2013.

2. Ibid.

3. "Smallpox Disease Overview." *Emergency Preparedness and Response*. CDC, 6 Feb. 2007. Web. 10 Apr. 2013.

4. "Why Vaccinate?" *The History of Vaccines*. The College of Physicians of Philadelphia, 2012. Web. 10 Apr. 2013.

5. "Progress Toward Immunization." *Living Proof Project*. Bill & Melinda Gates Foundation, Sept. 2009. Web. 10 Apr. 2013.

6. "What Would Happen If We Stopped Vaccinations?" *Vaccines and Immunization*. CDC, 20 Nov. 2012. Web. 10 Apr. 2013.

7. Ibid.

8. "Whole Populations To Be Vaccinated in Emergency Response To Polio Outbreak." *UNICEF*. UNICEF, 11 Nov. 2010. Web. 10 Apr. 2013.

9. "What Would Happen If We Stopped Vaccinations?" *Vaccines and Immunization*. CDC, 20 Nov. 2012. Web. 10 Apr. 2013.

Chapter 3. The Search for Vaccines

1. "Living Longer." *Global Health and Aging*. National Institutes of Health, 2011. Web. 21 Dec. 2012.

2. "Timelines." *The History of Vaccines*. The College of Physicians of Philadelphia, 2012. Web. 10 Apr. 2013.

3. Stefan Riedel. "Edward Jenner and the History of Smallpox and Vaccination." *Baylor University Medical Center*. US National Library of Medicine, Jan. 2005. Web. 10 Apr. 2013.

4. Ibid.

5. "Timelines." *The History of Vaccines*. The College of Physicians of Philadelphia, 2012. Web. 10 Apr. 2013.

6. Ibid.

7. "Achievements in Public Health, 1900–1999: Impact of Vaccines Universally Recommended for Children." *MMWR Weekly*. CDC, 2 Apr. 1999. Web. 10 Apr. 2013.

Chapter 4. Types of Vaccines

1. Robert W. Sears. *The Vaccine Book: Making the Right Decision for Your Child*. New York: Little, 2011. Print. 195.

2. April Cashin-Garbutt. "Malaria Vaccine Trial: An Interview with Professor Sir Brian Greenwood." *News Medical*. News Medical, 12 Dec. 2012. Web. 21 Dec. 2012.

3. "Vaccine Side Effects and Adverse Events." *The History of Vaccines*. The College of Physicians of Philadelphia, 2012. Web. 10 Apr. 2013.

Source Notes Continued

Chapter 5. Vaccines and Public Health

1. "Immunization and Infectious Disease." *HealthyPeople.gov*. US Department of Health and Human Services, 6 Sept. 2012. Web. 10 Apr. 2013.

2. Karen Rowan. "6 Flu Vaccine Myths." *Yahoo! News*. Yahoo! News, 26 Oct. 2012. Web. 13 Jan. 2013.

3. "Estimated Vaccination Coverage with Individual Vaccines and Selected Vaccination Series Before 24 Months of Age by State and Local Area." *Statistics and Surveillance: 2011 Table Data*. CDC. 2011. Web. 2 Jan. 2013.

4. "Vaccines for Teenagers." *The History of Vaccines*. The College of Physicians of Philadelphia, 2012. Web. 10 Apr. 2013.

5. "Achievements in Public Health, 1900–1999: Impact of Vaccines Universally Recommended for Children." *MMWR Weekly*. CDC, 2 Apr. 1999. Web. 10 Apr. 2013.

6. "Timelines." *The History of Vaccines*. The College of Physicians of Philadelphia, 2012. Web. 10 Apr. 2013.

7. Ibid.

8. "Measles Outbreaks." *CDC*. CDC, 2012. Web. 2 Jan. 2013.

9. "Value of Vaccines." *Global Health Program*. Bill & Melinda Gates Foundation, 2010. Web. 2 Jan. 2013.

10. "Progress Toward Immunization." *Living Proof Project*. Bill & Melinda Gates Foundation, Sept. 2009. Web. 10 Apr. 2013.

11. "The Bill & Melinda Gates Foundation." *GAVI Alliance*. GAVI Alliance, 2013. Web. 10 Apr. 2013.

12. "Value of Vaccines." *Global Health Program*. Bill & Melinda Gates Foundation, 2010. Web. 2 Jan. 2013.

13. "2010 Annual Letter from Bill Gates: The Miracle of Vaccines." *Who We Are*. Bill & Melinda Gates Foundation, 2010. Web. 10 Apr. 2013.

14. Peg Willingham. Shot@Life in Honduras: A Vaccination Success Story. *Shot@Life*. Bill & Melinda Gates Foundation, 12 Jan. 2012. Web. 3 Jan. 2013.

Chapter 6. The Process of Immunization

1. "Notice to Readers: Guidelines for Maintaining and Managing the Vaccine Cold Chain." *MMWR Weekly*. CDC, 24 Oct. 2003. Web. 4 Jan. 2013.

2. "Bill and Melinda Gates Pledge $10 Billion in Call for Decade of Vaccines." *Bill & Melinda Gates Foundation*. Bill & Melinda Gates Foundation, 29 Jan. 2010. Web. 4 Jan. 2013.

Chapter 7. The Anti-Vaccine Controversy

1. Mark A. Largent. *Vaccine: The Debate in Modern America*. Baltimore, MD: Johns Hopkins UP, 2012. Print. 32–34, 38.

2. "History of Anti-Vaccination Movements." *The History of Vaccines*. The College of Physicians of Philadelphia, 2012. Web. 10 Apr. 2013.

3. Tim O'Shea. "A Primer on Vaccination vs. Immunization." *Weeks MD*. Weeks MD, 8 Oct. 2009. Web. 28 May 2013.

4. Robert W. Sears. *The Vaccine Book: Making the Right Decision for Your Child*. New York: Little, 2011. Print. 229–231.

5. Daniel R. Bronfin. "Childhood Immunization Controversies: What Are Parents Asking?" *Ochsner J*. US National Library of Medicine, Fall 2008. Web. 10 Apr. 2013.

6. "Who and When." *Vaccines.gov*. US Department of Health and Human Services, 2012. Web. 10 Jan. 2013.

Chapter 8. Vaccines of Tomorrow

1. G. J. Nossal. "Vaccines of the Future." *PubMed.gov*. US National Library of Medicine, 2011. Web. 13 Dec. 2012.

2. "The Development of HIV Vaccines." *The History of Vaccines*. The College of Physicians of Philadelphia, 2012. Web. 10 Apr. 2013.

3. Ibid.

4. "The Future of Immunization." *The History of Vaccines*. The College of Physicians of Philadelphia, 2012. Web. 10 Apr. 2013.

5. "Biological Weapons, Bioterrorism, and Vaccines." *The History of Vaccines*. The College of Physicians of Philadelphia, 2012. Web. 10 Apr. 2013.

6. Ibid.

Index

About the Author

Carol Hand has a PhD in zoology. She has taught college biology, written biology assessments and middle school and high school science curricula, and authored a dozen young-adult science books. Currently she works as a freelance science writer.

About the Consultant

Jonah Sacha received his PhD in Microbiology & Immunology from the University of Wisconsin–Madison in 2007. He is currently an assistant professor at Oregon Health & Science University, where he leads a vaccine research and development team.